ADVANCED DUNGEONS & DYNAMICS 365 IMPLEMENTATION GUIDE

THE WATERDEEP TRADING COMPANY PROJECT

MODULE 3: CONFIGURING A NEW COMPANY WITHIN DYNAMICS 365

MURRAY FIFE

www.dynamicscompanions.com
Dynamics Companions

- 1 -

www.blindsquirrelpublishing.com
© 2019 Blind Squirrel Publishing, LLC , All Rights Reserved

BLIND SQUIRREL
PUBLISHING

ISBN-13: 978-1077207929

www.dynamicscompanions.com
Dynamics Companions

- 2 -

www.blindsquirrelpublishing.com
© 2019 Blind Squirrel Publishing, LLC , All Rights Reserved

BLIND SQUIRREL
PUBLISHING

Preface

I have been reviving an old project that started a while ago and have started up a new project blog to track the progress. Being a lifelong fan of Dungeons & Dragons, with the unfortunate problem that I cannot find anyone to play with I have decided to create a test implementation Dynamics 365 in the AD&D format just to see how it would work and if I can find some creative ways to use Dynamics 365 and chose to implement the **Waterdeep Trading Company** as an example where I can track their many legal (and not so legal) entities within Faerûn.

dync
www.dynamicscompanions.com
Dynamics Companions

- 3 -

www.blindsquirrelpublishing.com
© 2019 Blind Squirrel Publishing, LLC , All Rights Reserved

BLIND SQUIRREL
PUBLISHING

Table of Contents

dync
www.dynamicscompanions.com
Dynamics Companions

- 5 -

www.blindsquirrelpublishing.com
© 2019 Blind Squirrel Publishing, LLC , All Rights Reserved

BLIND SQUIRREL
PUBLISHING

Introduction

For us to track all the financial and operational information for the **Waterdeep Trading Company**, we will need to set up a new company within Dynamics 365 with its own financial ledger. Additionally, we will probably want to track all our money through a bank account or two.

This company will be the foundation for all the other functions that we will build later, like the inventory management, sales, procurement and more.

BLIND SQUIRREL
PUBLISHING

Configuring a new Company for the Waterdeep Trading Company

Although the **Waterdeep Trading Company** has several different operations that they are managing, the one that they decided to focus on initially was the most public one, and that is the **Waterdeep Trading Company** retail store and inventory management operations.

In this module, we will set up a new company for the **Waterdeep Trading Company**, along with its very own chart of accounts and register the operating bank account where we will track all our coinage.

Topics Covered

- Creating a new Legal Entity

- Configuring the Number Sequences for the Legal Entity

- Importing a standard Chart of Accounts

- Creating a new Account structure the Waterdeep Trading Company

- Configuring the Ledger for the Waterdeep Trading Company

- Creating an Operating Bank Account

- Setting the Waterdeep Trading Company as the default legal entity

- Summary

Creating a new Legal Entity

Dynamics 365 allows us to set up multiple companies within the one environment, broken out by **Legal Entities**. These can operate independently with their own financials, or they can share information between themselves for intercompany planning and even financial consolidations.

We can set these **Legal entities** up at the beginning of the implementation, and we can add additional Legal entities later as other businesses are acquired.

Topics Covered

- Opening the Legal entities maintenance form

- Creating a new Legal entity

- Updating the Address

- Updating the Legal Entities Banner

- Switching to the Waterdeep Trading Company legal entity

- Review

dync
www.dynamicscompanions.com
Dynamics Companions

- 9 -

www.blindsquirrelpublishing.com
© 2019 Blind Squirrel Publishing, LLC , All Rights Reserved

BLIND SQUIRREL
PUBLISHING

Opening the Legal entities maintenance form

To create a new Legal entity in the system, we will need to find the **Legal entity** maintenance form which tracks all the different companies and configurations in the system.

How to do it...

Step 1: Open the Legal entities form through the menu search

We can find the **Legal entities** form is through the menu search feature.

Type in **legal** into the menu search and select **Legal entities**.

dync
www.dynamicscompanions.com
Dynamics Companions

- 10 -

www.blindsquirrelpublishing.com
© 2019 Blind Squirrel Publishing, LLC , All Rights Reserved

BLIND SQUIRREL
PUBLISHING

Opening the Legal entities maintenance form

How to do it...

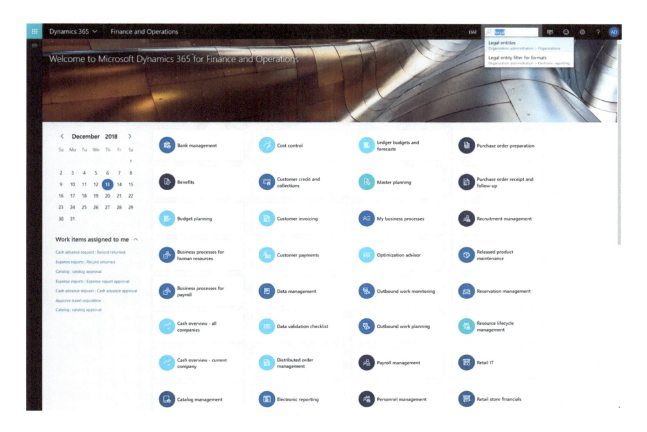

Step 1: Open the Legal entities form through the menu search

We can find the **Legal entities** form is through the menu search feature.

We can do this by clicking on the search icon in the header of the form (or by pressing **ALT+G**) and then type in **legal** into the search box. Then you will be able to select the **Legal entities** form from the dropdown list.

dync
dynamics companions

www.dynamicscompanions.com
Dynamics Companions

- 11 -

www.blindsquirrelpublishing.com
© 2019 Blind Squirrel Publishing, LLC , All Rights Reserved

BLIND SQUIRREL
PUBLISHING

Opening the Legal entities maintenance form

How to do it...

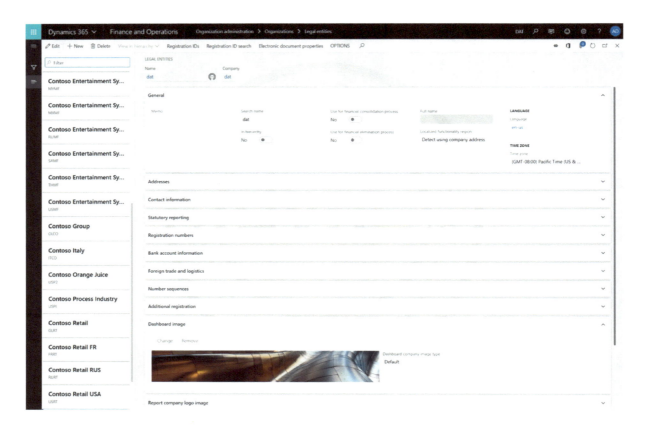

Step 1: Open the Legal entities form through the menu search

This will open the **Legal entities** maintenance form where we will be able to see any existing legal entities that are built into the current environment.

Creating a new Legal entity

Now we will want to create a new **Legal entity** for the **Waterdeep Trading Company**.

How to do it...

Step 1: Click on the New button

To do this, we will want to add a new **Legal entity** record into the system.

Click on the **New** button.

Step 2: Update the Name

We will start off by giving our new legal entity a full name to describe it.

Set the Name to Waterdeep Trading Company.

Step 3: Update the Company

We will then want to give our legal entity a **Company** code that we will use to reference it within the system.

Set the **Company** to **WDTC**.

Step 4: Choose the Country/region

And finally, we will want to select the country or region that this company is operating out of.

Click on the **Country/region** dropdown list And select **FAE**.

Step 5: Click on the OK button

After we have provided this little bit of information about our new company we can go ahead and create the Legal entity.

Click on the **OK** button.

Creating a new Legal entity

How to do it...

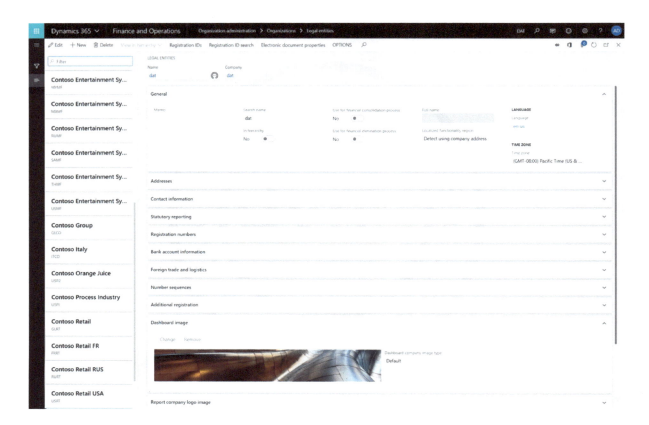

Step 1: Click on the New button

To do this, we will want to add a new **Legal entity** record into the system.

To do this just click on the **New** button.

Creating a new Legal entity

How to do it...

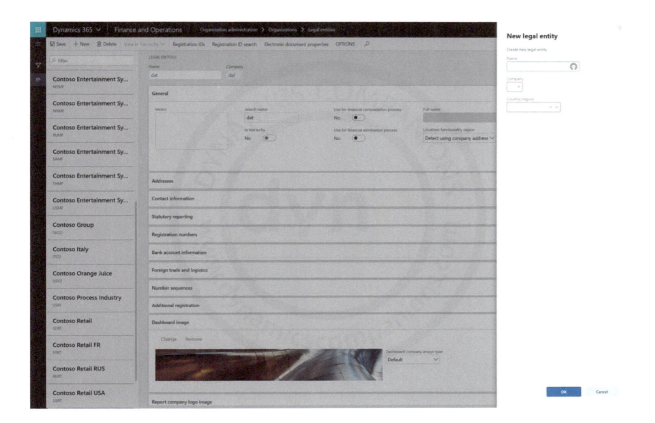

Step 1: Click on the New button

This will open the **New legal entity** dialog panel where we just need to provide a little bit of information about the new legal entity.

www.dynamicscompanions.com
Dynamics Companions

- 15 -

www.blindsquirrelpublishing.com
© 2019 Blind Squirrel Publishing, LLC , All Rights Reserved

BLIND SQUIRREL
PUBLISHING

Creating a new Legal entity

How to do it...

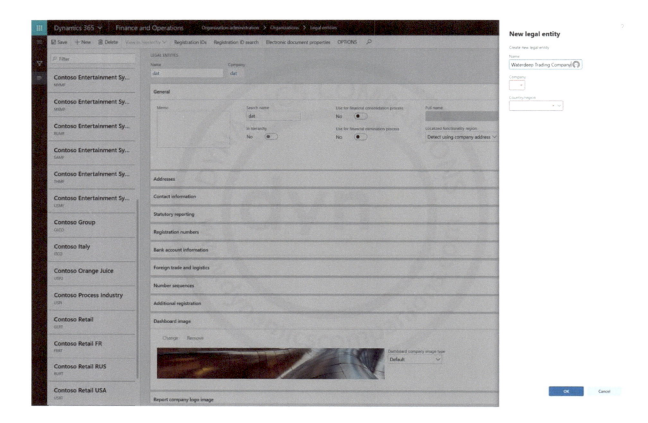

Step 2: Update the Name

We will start off by giving our new legal entity a full name to describe it.

To do this, we will just need to change the **Name** value.

This time, we will want to set the **Name** to **Waterdeep Trading Company**.

Creating a new Legal entity

How to do it...

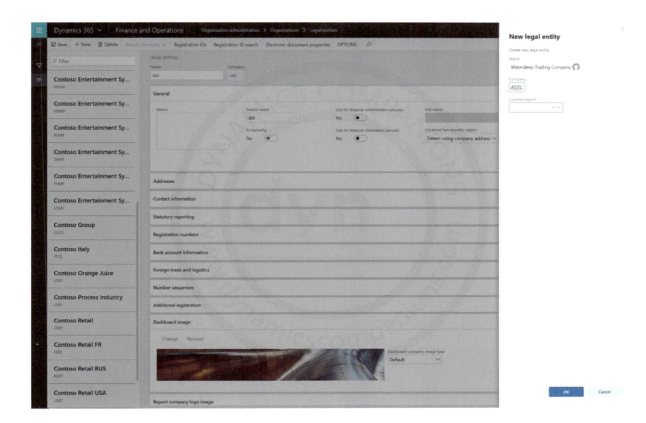

Step 3: Update the Company

We will then want to give our legal entity a **Company** code that we will use to reference it within the system.

To do this, we will just need to update the **Company** value.

This time, we will want to set the **Company** to **WDTC**.

dync
www.dynamicscompanions.com
Dynamics Companions

- 17 -

www.blindsquirrelpublishing.com
© 2019 Blind Squirrel Publishing, LLC , All Rights Reserved

BLIND SQUIRREL
PUBLISHING

Creating a new Legal entity

How to do it...

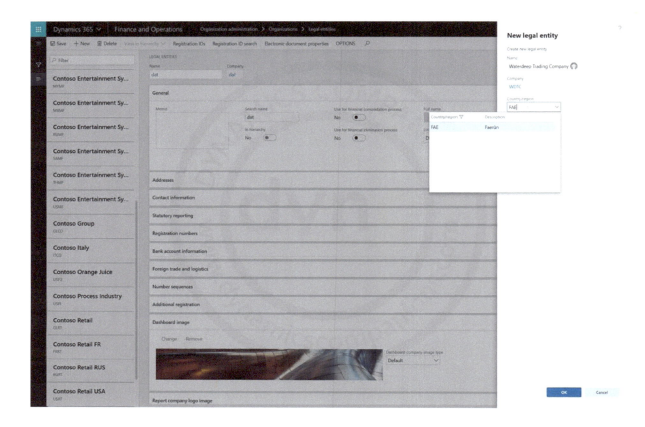

Step 4: Choose the Country/region

And finally, we will want to select the country or region that this company is operating out of.

Luckily for us, since we have set up the Faerûn localization in the previous step, we are able to choose **Faerûn** as the country.

To do this just pick the **Country/region** option from the dropdown list.

For this example, we will want to click on the **Country/region** dropdown list and pick **FAE**.

dync
www.dynamicscompanions.com
Dynamics Companions

- 18 -

www.blindsquirrelpublishing.com
© 2019 Blind Squirrel Publishing, LLC , All Rights Reserved

BLIND SQUIRREL
PUBLISHING

Creating a new Legal entity

How to do it...

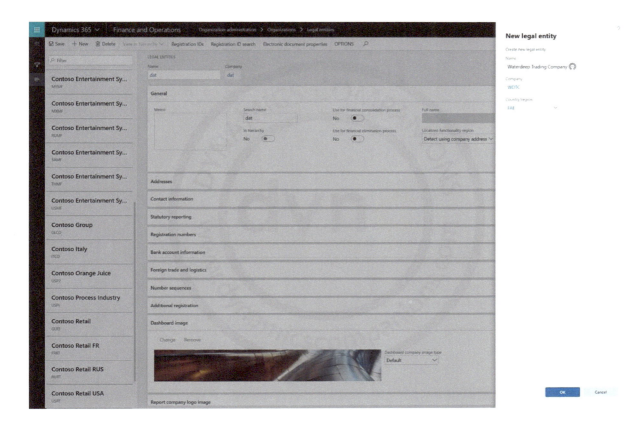

Step 5: Click on the OK button

After we have provided this little bit of information about our new company we can go ahead and create the Legal entity.

To do this, all we need to do is click on the **OK** button.

Creating a new Legal entity

How to do it...

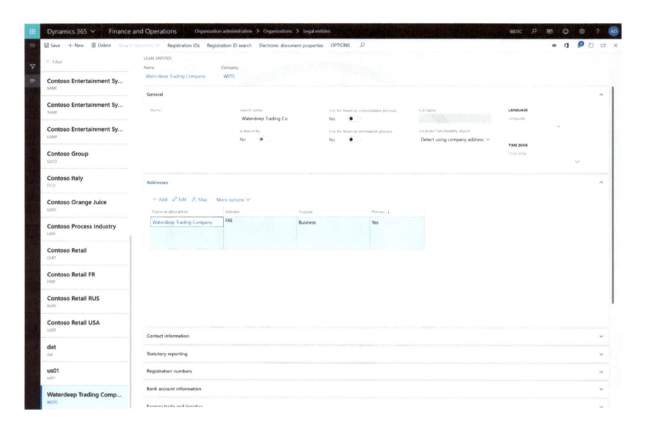

Step 5: Click on the OK button

This will take us back to the main view of the **Legal entities,** and we will now have a new Legal entity for the **Waterdeep Trading Company**.

Updating the Address

Now that we have a new legal entity for the **Waterdeep Trading Company** we can make a couple of tweaks to the default details. We will start off by updating the corporate address.

How to do it...

Step 1: Click on the Edit button

We already have an address that is associated with our new Legal entity, but it doesn't have any details other than the country code.

So we will want to edit that default address.

Click on the **Edit** button within the **Addresses** section.

Step 2: Update the Street

We will start off by updating the street address for the **Waterdeep Trading Company.**

Set the Street to 1 Merchant Way.

Step 3: Select the City

Next, we will want to select the city that the company operates out of.

Click on the **City** dropdown list And choose **Waterdeep**.

Step 4: Click on the OK button

After we selected one of the standard addresses, we will see that the State defaults in from the city information.

That should do the setup of the address details, and we can save the address details.

Click on the **OK** button.

Updating the Address

How to do it...

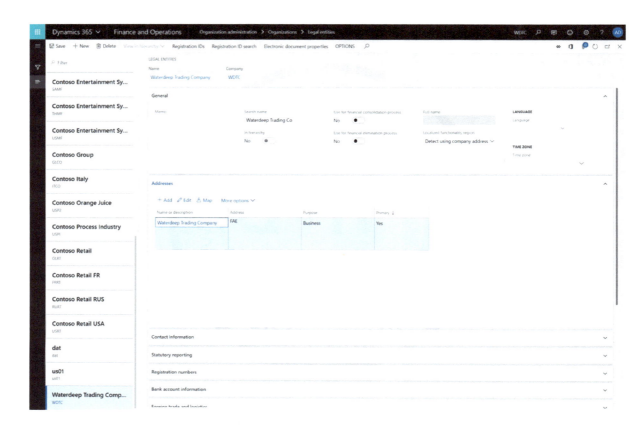

Step 1: Click on the Edit button

We already have an address that is associated with our new Legal entity, but it doesn't have any details other than the country code.

So we will want to edit that default address.

To do this, all we need to do is click on the **Edit** button within the **Addresses** section.

dync
Dynamics Companions

www.dynamicscompanions.com
Dynamics Companions

- 22 -

www.blindsquirrelpublishing.com
© 2019 Blind Squirrel Publishing, LLC , All Rights Reserved

BLIND SQUIRREL
PUBLISHING

Updating the Address

How to do it...

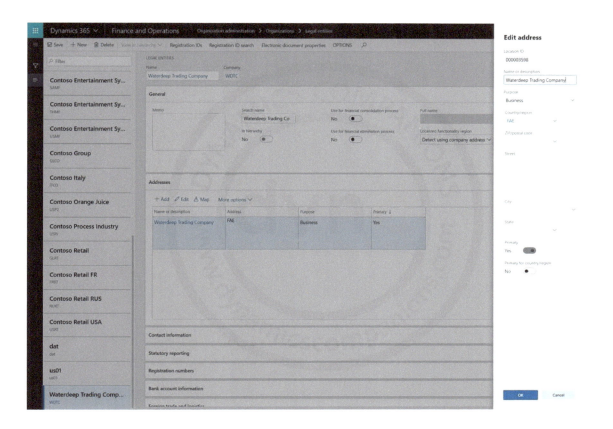

Step 1: Click on the Edit button

This will open an **Edit address** panel which will allow us to update the address details for the legal entity.

www.dynamicscompanions.com
Dynamics Companions

- 23 -

www.blindsquirrelpublishing.com
© 2019 Blind Squirrel Publishing, LLC , All Rights Reserved

BLIND SQUIRREL
PUBLISHING

Updating the Address

How to do it...

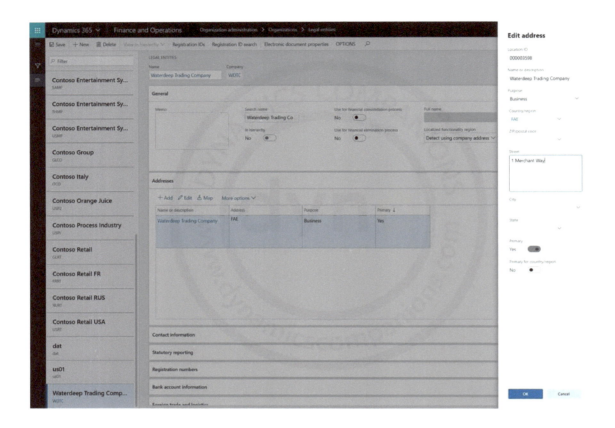

Step 2: Update the Street

We will start off by updating the street address for the **Waterdeep Trading Company.**

To do this, we will just need to change the **Street** value.

For this example, we will want to set the **Street** to **1 Merchant Way**.

Updating the Address

How to do it...

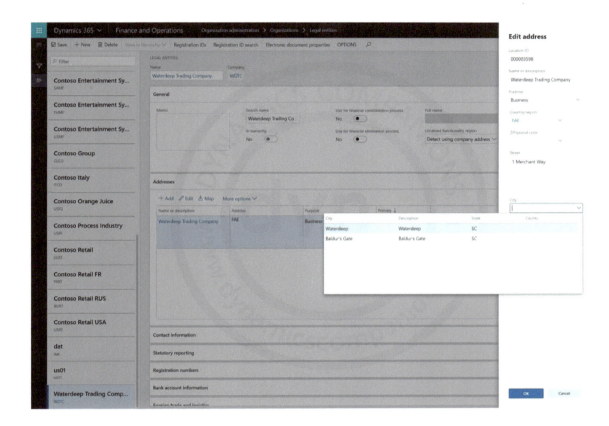

Step 3: Select the City

Next, we will want to select the city that the company operates out of.

Since we added some cities into the address details for Faerûn, these will show up in the drop-down box. We are not limited to just these addresses; we can also just type in an address if we need to.

To do this just pick the **City** option from the dropdown list.

For this example, we will want to click on the **City** dropdown list and pick **Waterdeep**.

dync
www.dynamicscompanions.com
Dynamics Companions

- 25 -

www.blindsquirrelpublishing.com
© 2019 Blind Squirrel Publishing, LLC , All Rights Reserved

BLIND SQUIRREL
PUBLISHING

Updating the Address

How to do it...

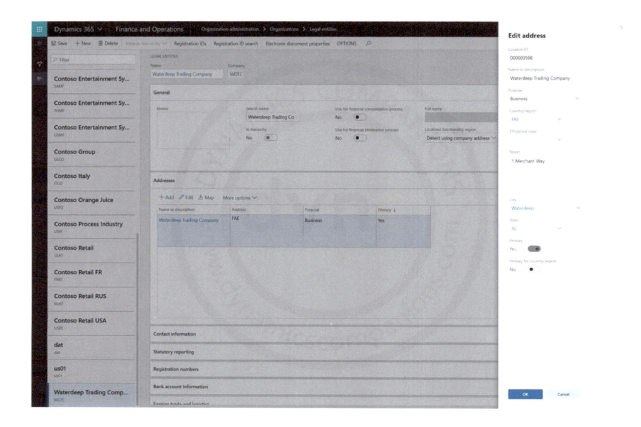

Step 4: Click on the OK button

After we selected one of the standard addresses, we will see that the State defaults in from the city information.

That should do the setup of the address details, and we can save the address details.

To do this, all we need to do is click on the **OK** button.

dync
www.dynamicscompanions.com
Dynamics Companions

- 26 -

www.blindsquirrelpublishing.com
© 2019 Blind Squirrel Publishing, LLC , All Rights Reserved

BLIND SQUIRREL
PUBLISHING

Updating the Address

How to do it...

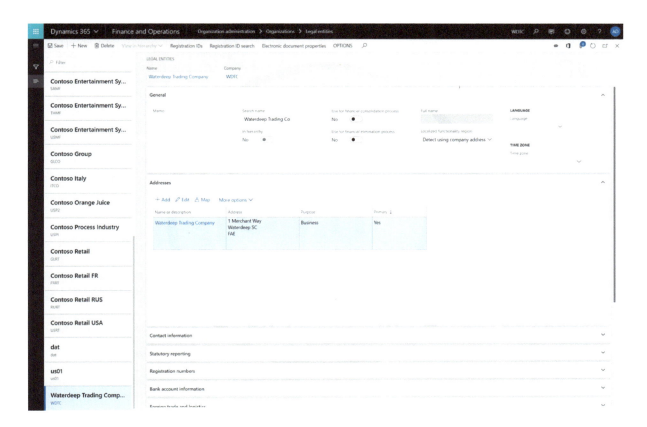

Step 4: Click on the OK button

When we return to the Legal entity, we will see that the address information looks a lot better than before.

Updating the Legal Entities Banner

Dynamics 365 has a feature that allows us to have different banners that show on the main dashboard, that we can personalize to the current legal entity that we are in.

To make the **Waterdeep Trading Company** a little more personalized, and to help us identify the company that we are working in, we will quickly update the banner to brand it to the company.

How to do it...

Step 1: Expand the Dashboard images tab group

We can see the default banner details within the **Dashboard images** section of the legal entity record.

Expand the **Dashboard images** tab group.

Step 2: Select the Dashboard company image type

By default, the dashboard image that is shown is the Default image that is used in every version of Dynamics 365.

We will want to tell the system that we want to use a custom banner.

Click on the **Dashboard company image type** dropdown list And select **Banner**.

Step 3: Click on the Change button

Now we will want to change the default image that is associated with the legal entity record.

Click on the **Change** button.

Step 4: Click on the Browse button

This will open the **Select image file to upload** dialog panel, and we will want to select a new banner image.

Click on the **Browse** button.

Step 5: Click on the Open button

Now we can just browse to the new banner image that we want to use and select it.

Click on the **Open** button.

Updating the Legal Entities Banner

How to do it...

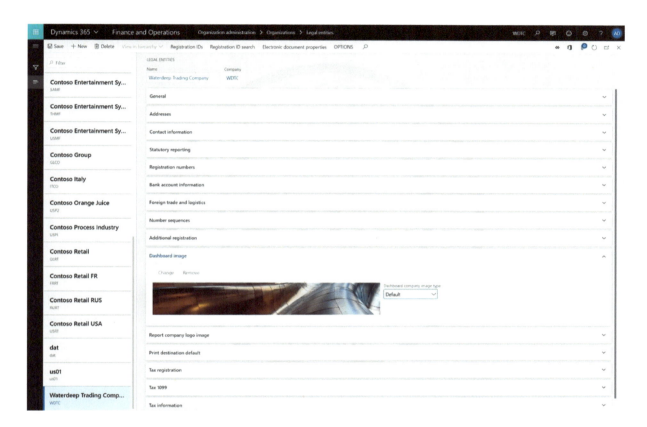

Step 1: Expand the Dashboard images tab group

We can see the default banner details within the **Dashboard images** section of the legal entity record.

To do this, all we need to do is expand the **Dashboard images** tab group.

www.dynamicscompanions.com
Dynamics Companions

- 29 -

www.blindsquirrelpublishing.com
© 2019 Blind Squirrel Publishing, LLC , All Rights Reserved

BLIND SQUIRREL
PUBLISHING

dync

Updating the Legal Entities Banner

How to do it...

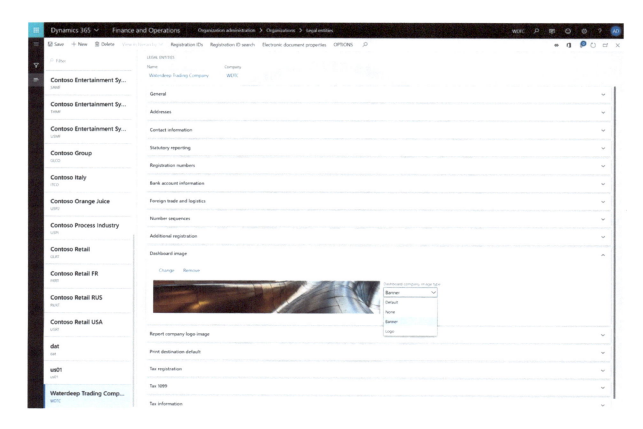

Step 2: Select the Dashboard company image type

By default, the dashboard image that is shown is the Default image that is used in every version of Dynamics 365.

We will want to tell the system that we want to use a custom banner.

To do this just pick the **Dashboard company image type** value from the dropdown list.

This time, we will want to click on the **Dashboard company image type** dropdown list and pick **Banner**.

dync
www.dynamicscompanions.com
Dynamics Companions

- 30 -

www.blindsquirrelpublishing.com
© 2019 Blind Squirrel Publishing, LLC , All Rights Reserved

BLIND SQUIRREL
PUBLISHING

Updating the Legal Entities Banner

How to do it...

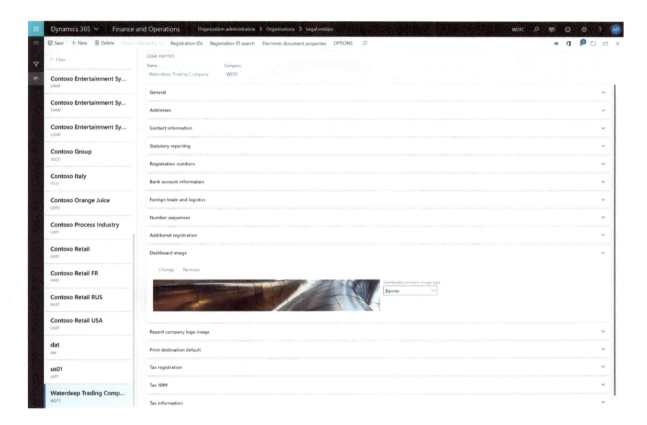

Step 3: Click on the Change button

Now we will want to change the default image that is associated with the legal entity record.

To do this just click on the **Change** button.

dync
dynamics companions

www.dynamicscompanions.com
Dynamics Companions

- 31 -

www.blindsquirrelpublishing.com
© 2019 Blind Squirrel Publishing, LLC , All Rights Reserved

BLIND SQUIRREL
PUBLISHING

Updating the Legal Entities Banner

How to do it...

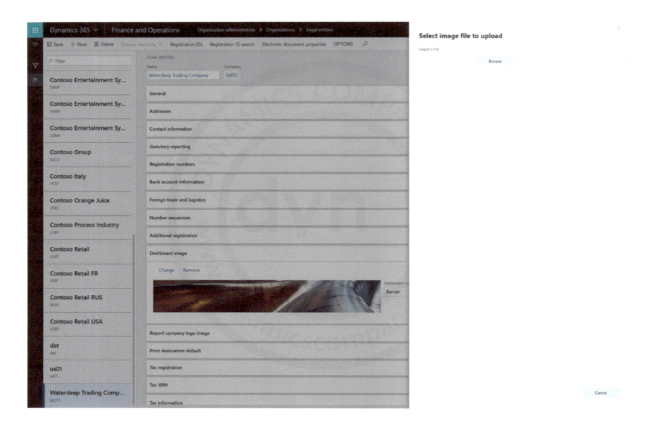

Step 4: Click on the Browse button

This will open the **Select image file to upload** dialog panel, and we will want to select a new banner image.

To do this just click on the **Browse** button.

Updating the Legal Entities Banner

How to do it...

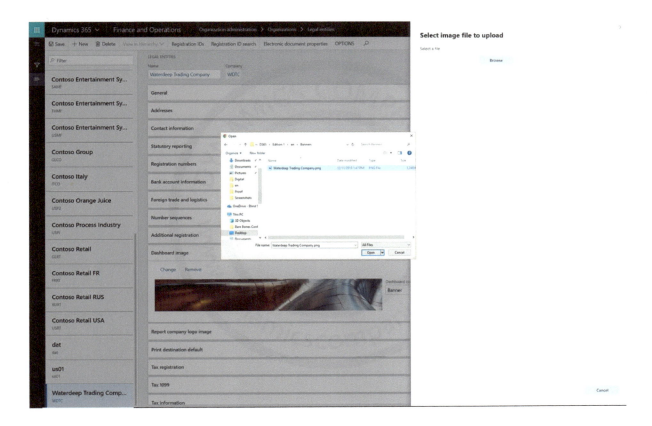

Step 5: Click on the Open button

Now we can just browse to the new banner image that we want to use and select it.

To do this, all we need to do is click on the **Open** button.

Updating the Legal Entities Banner

How to do it...

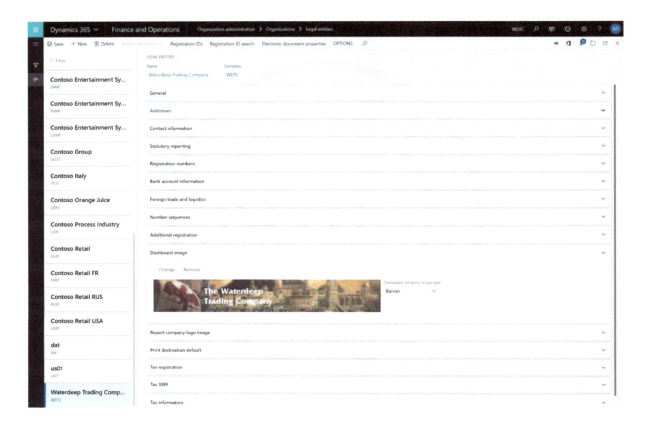

Step 5: Click on the Open button

This will upload the image and show us the new banner in the **Dashboard image** section of the legal entity record.

Switching to the Waterdeep Trading Company legal entity

Now that we have created our new **Legal entity** for the **Waterdeep Trading Company** we can switch our company from the default **DAT** company to the **WDTC** company.

How to do it...

Step 1: Select the Company

To do this, we will just want to select our new **WDTC** company code from the list of companies in the system.

Click on the **Company** dropdown list And select **WDTC**.

Switching to the Waterdeep Trading Company legal entity

How to do it...

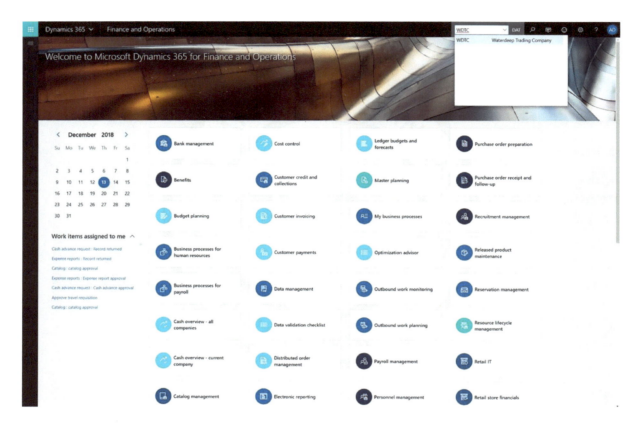

Step 1: Select the Company

To do this, we will just want to select our new **WDTC** company code from the list of companies in the system.

To do this just pick the **Company** value from the dropdown list.

This time, we will want to click on the **Company** dropdown list and select **WDTC**.

www.dynamicscompanions.com
Dynamics Companions

- 36 -

www.blindsquirrelpublishing.com
© 2019 Blind Squirrel Publishing, LLC , All Rights Reserved

BLIND SQUIRREL
PUBLISHING

Switching to the Waterdeep Trading Company legal entity

How to do it...

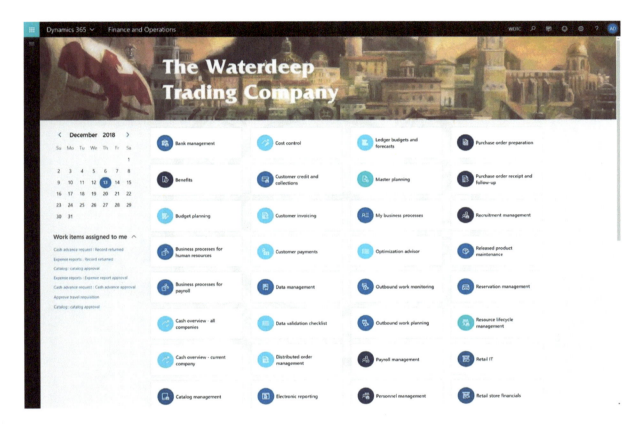

Step 1: Select the Company

After we have done that, we will see the new banner for the **Waterdeep Trading Company** which will tell us that we have switched companies.

dync
dynamics companions
www.dynamicscompanions.com
Dynamics Companions

- 37 -

www.blindsquirrelpublishing.com
© 2019 Blind Squirrel Publishing, LLC , All Rights Reserved

BLIND SQUIRREL
PUBLISHING

Review

How easy was that? We now have a new Legal Entity for the **Waterdeep Trading Company** that we can start configuring.

Configuring the Number Sequences for the Legal Entity

Each Legal entity within Dynamics 365 can have its own unique set of number sequences that it used to number Journals, Order, even Customers, and Products.

We can set these up individually, or we can get the system to create the default number sequences and associate them with the default number sequence options in the system.

Before we move on, we will need to set these up, and we will take the easy route and have Dynamics 365 create all the number sequences for us.

Topics Covered

- Opening the Number sequences maintenance form

- Generating the number sequences with the Number sequence wizard

- Review

Opening the Number sequences maintenance form

To do this we will need to find the Number sequence maintenance form.

How to do it...

Step 1: Open the Number sequences form through the menu search

We can find the **Number sequences** form is through the menu search feature.

Type in **number se** into the menu search and select **Number sequences**.

Opening the Number sequences maintenance form

How to do it...

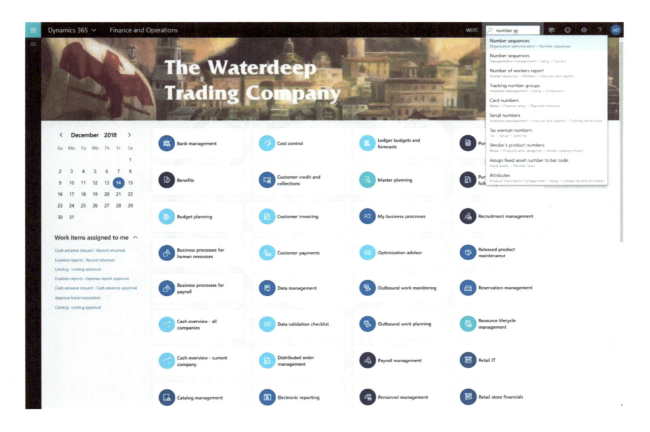

Step 1: Open the Number sequences form through the menu search

We can find the **Number sequences** form is through the menu search feature.

We can do this by clicking on the search icon in the header of the form (or by pressing **ALT+G**) and then type in **number se** into the search box. Then you will be able to select the **Number sequences** form from the dropdown list.

dync
www.dynamicscompanions.com
Dynamics Companions

- 41 -

www.blindsquirrelpublishing.com
© 2019 Blind Squirrel Publishing, LLC , All Rights Reserved

BLIND SQUIRREL
PUBLISHING

Opening the Number sequences maintenance form

How to do it...

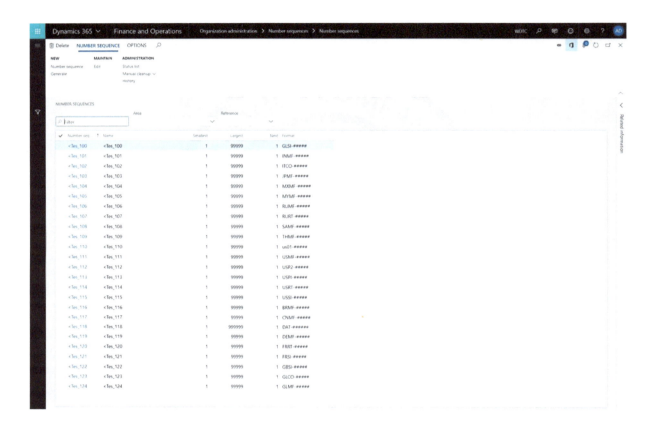

Step 1: Open the Number sequences form through the menu search

This will open the **Number sequences** maintenance form where we will see all the existing number sequences for the other companies.

dync
dynamics companions

www.dynamicscompanions.com
Dynamics Companions

- 42 -

www.blindsquirrelpublishing.com
© 2019 Blind Squirrel Publishing, LLC , All Rights Reserved

BLIND SQUIRREL PUBLISHING

Generating the number sequences with the Number sequence wizard

Now we will use the number sequence wizard to do all the hard work for us.

How to do it...

Step 1: Click on the Generate button

To do this, we will kick off the automatic Number sequence generation wizard,

Click on the **Generate** button.

Step 2: Click on the Next button

This will open the **Set up number sequences** wizard, and we will want to step through the default options.

Click on the **Next** button.

Step 3: Click on the Next button

On the second page of the wizard, we will see all the new number sequences that it is suggesting that we create. They look good to us, so we can just continue on.

Click on the **Next** button.

Step 4: Click on the Finish button

On the final page of the wizard, we will get a summary of all the different number sequences that are being created by module, and we can tell the system to build them all for us.

Click on the **Finish** button.

Generating the number sequences with the Number sequence wizard

How to do it...

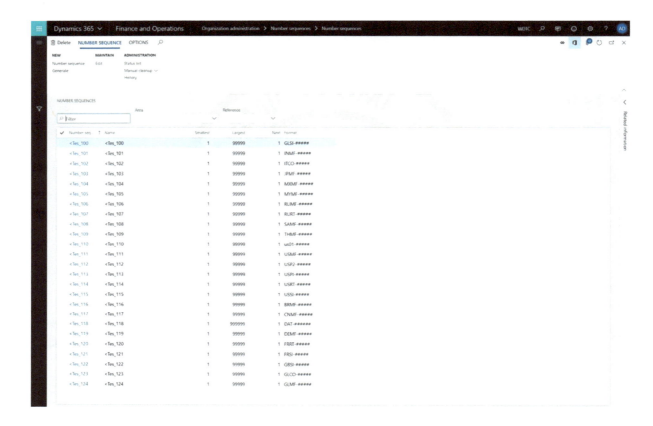

Step 1: Click on the Generate button

To do this, we will kick off the automatic Number sequence generation wizard,

To do this, all we need to do is click on the **Generate** button.

Generating the number sequences with the Number sequence wizard

How to do it...

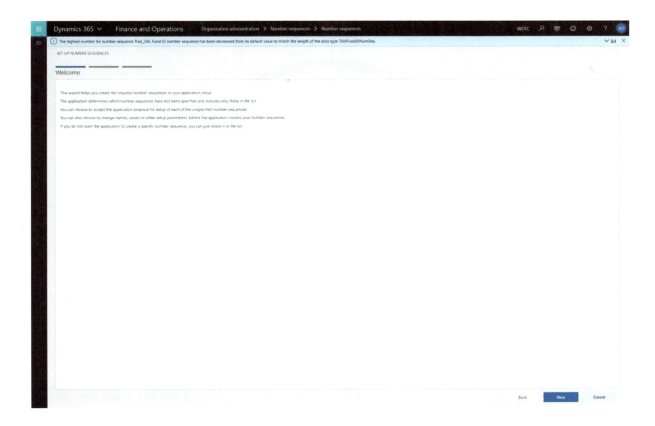

Step 2: Click on the Next button

This will open the **Set up number sequences** wizard, and we will want to step through the default options.

To do this just click on the **Next** button.

www.dynamicscompanions.com
Dynamics Companions

- 45 -

www.blindsquirrelpublishing.com
© 2019 Blind Squirrel Publishing, LLC , All Rights Reserved

BLIND SQUIRREL
PUBLISHING

Generating the number sequences with the Number sequence wizard

How to do it...

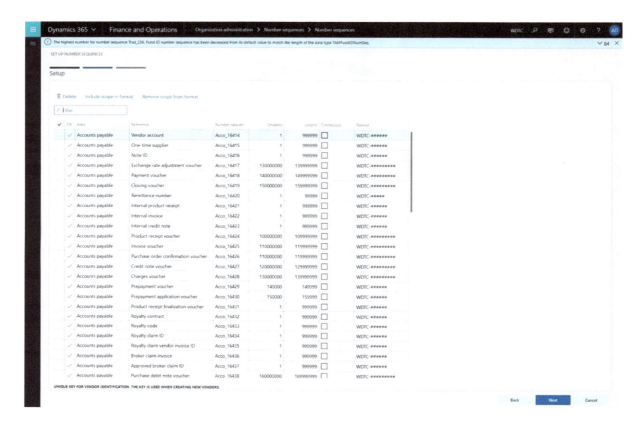

Step 3: Click on the Next button

On the second page of the wizard, we will see all the new number sequences that it is suggesting that we create. They look good to us, so we can just continue on.

To do this, all we need to do is click on the **Next** button.

dync
www.dynamicscompanions.com
Dynamics Companions

- 46 -

www.blindsquirrelpublishing.com
© 2019 Blind Squirrel Publishing, LLC , All Rights Reserved

BLIND SQUIRREL
PUBLISHING

Generating the number sequences with the Number sequence wizard

How to do it...

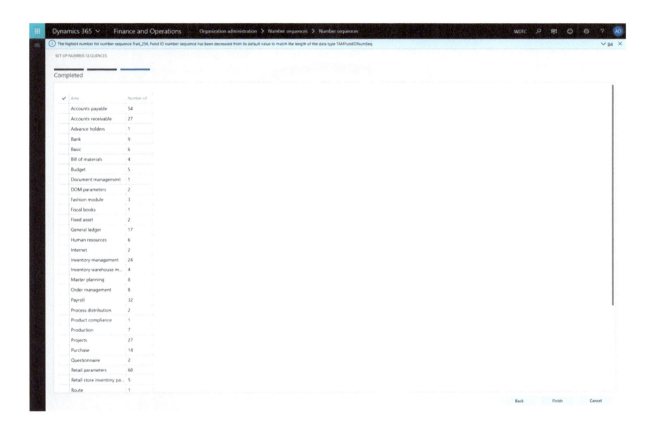

Step 4: Click on the Finish button

On the final page of the wizard, we will get a summary of all the different number sequences that are being created by module, and we can tell the system to build them all for us.

To do this just click on the **Finish** button.

Generating the number sequences with the Number sequence wizard

How to do it...

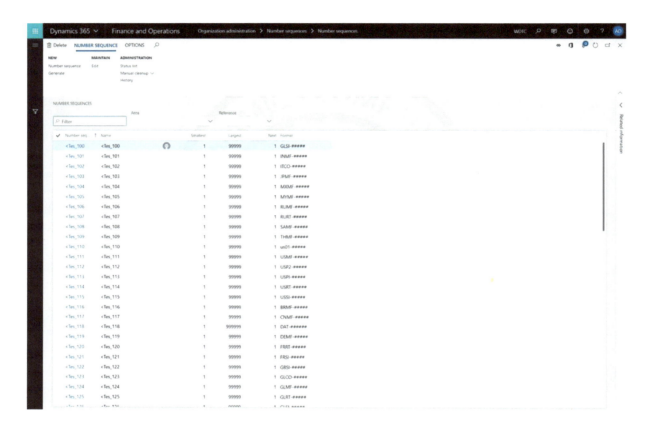

Step 4: Click on the Finish button

That will return us to the **Number sequence** maintenance form, and we are done with the setup.

dync
www.dynamicscompanions.com
Dynamics Companions

- 48 -

www.blindsquirrelpublishing.com
© 2019 Blind Squirrel Publishing, LLC , All Rights Reserved

BLIND SQUIRREL
PUBLISHING

Review

How easy was that? We definitely don't want to build all those number sequences by hand, so the number sequence generation wizard is a huge timesaver.

Importing a standard Chart of Accounts

Now that we have our new legal entity, we will want to set up some of the financial information for the **Waterdeep Trading Company.**

We will start off by creating a simple Chart of Accounts that we will use as our standard Chart of Accounts for all our Faerûn legal entities.

We could do this by hand and enter in all the main accounts, but we are lucky to have an import package that has all the standard accounts for us that is used throughout Faerûn so we will just import that using the data management tools.

Topics Covered

- Opening up the Data Management workspace

- Importing the Faerûn Chart of Accounts

- Viewing the Standard Chart of Accounts

- Review

Opening up the Data Management workspace

To import the new Chard of Accounts we will want to open the **Data Management** Workspace.

How to do it...

Step 1: Open the Data management form through the menu search

We can find the **Data management** form is through the menu search feature.

Type in **data man** into the menu search and select **Data management**.

Step 2: Click on the Close button

This will take us to the Data management workspace. Since this is the first time that we are using the data management tools, we will get a notice that it is building all the data entities for us which is what we use to import in all our data.

We will just want to wait a few minutes for this to build.

Click on the **Close** button.

Opening up the Data Management workspace

How to do it...

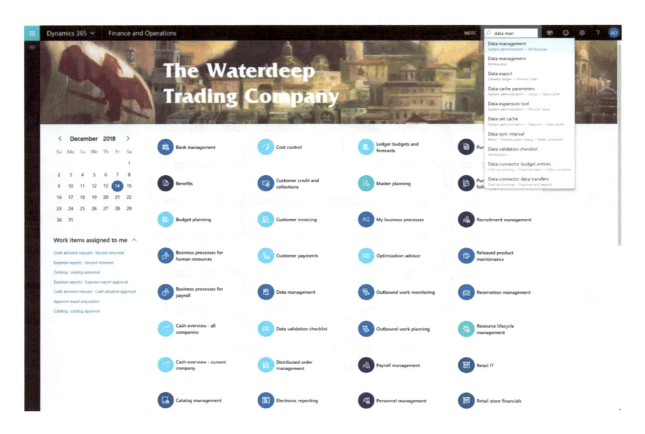

Step 1: Open the Data management form through the menu search

We can find the **Data management** form is through the menu search feature.

We can do this by clicking on the search icon in the header of the form (or by pressing **ALT+G**) and then type in **data man** into the search box. Then you will be able to select the **Data management** form from the dropdown list.

dync
www.dynamicscompanions.com
Dynamics Companions

- 52 -

www.blindsquirrelpublishing.com
© 2019 Blind Squirrel Publishing, LLC , All Rights Reserved

BLIND SQUIRREL
PUBLISHING

Opening up the Data Management workspace

How to do it...

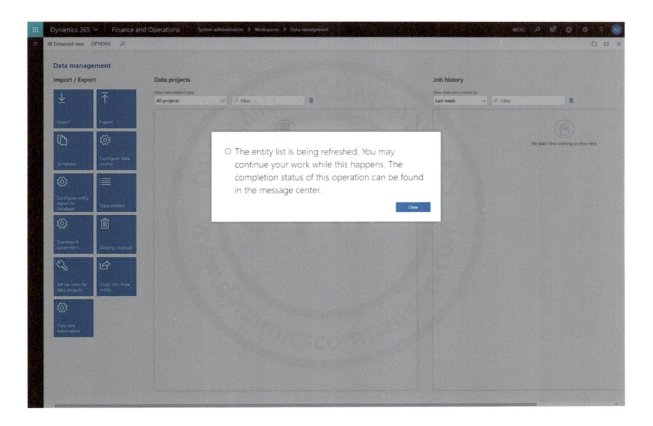

Step 2: Click on the Close button

This will take us to the Data management workspace. Since this is the first time that we are using the data management tools, we will get a notice that it is building all the data entities for us which is what we use to import in all our data.

We will just want to wait a few minutes for this to build.

To do this just click on the **Close** button.

www.dynamicscompanions.com
Dynamics Companions

- 53 -

www.blindsquirrelpublishing.com
© 2019 Blind Squirrel Publishing, LLC , All Rights Reserved

BLIND SQUIRREL
PUBLISHING

Opening up the Data Management workspace

How to do it...

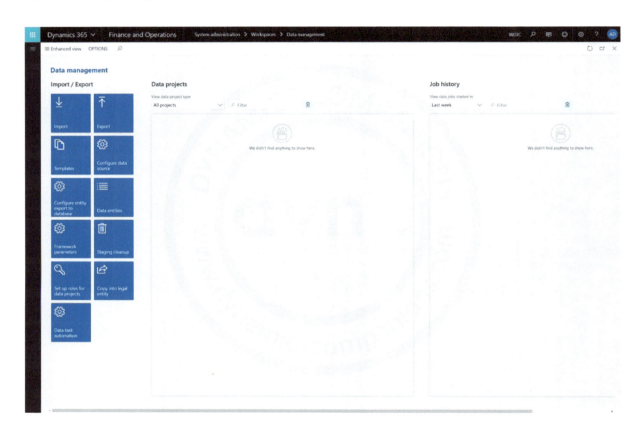

Step 2: Click on the Close button

After a few minutes, we will get a notice that the data entities have been built and we can move on.

www.dynamicscompanions.com
Dynamics Companions

- 54 -

www.blindsquirrelpublishing.com
© 2019 Blind Squirrel Publishing, LLC , All Rights Reserved

BLIND SQUIRREL
PUBLISHING

Importing the Faerûn Chart of Accounts

Now we will use the Data Management Import feature to import in our standard Chard of Accounts.

How to do it...

Step 1: Click on the Import button

To do this, we just create a new import job.

Click on the **Import** button.

Step 2: Update the Name

We will start off by giving our import job a unique name to identify the import.

Set the Name to WDTCStandardCOA.

Step 3: Choose the Source data format

We will be importing the chart of accounts data using a zipped-up package that contains all the different entities that we need to set up the Chart of Accounts, so we will want to specify that the import is a Package format.

Click on the **Source data format** dropdown list And select **Package**.

Step 4: Click on the Upload button

Next, we will want to upload the data import package.

Click on the **Upload** button.

Step 5: Click on the Open button

When the File explorer dialog is opened, we just need to navigate to the data package and open it.

Click on the **Open** button.

Step 6: Click on the Import button

If we are in the **Enhanced view,** then it will look a little different, but we will still see that there are eleven different entities that are being imported by this package.

All we need to do now is start the import process.

Click on the **Import** button.

Step 7: Click on the Close button

This will start off a batch job that will import the data in the package for us.

Click on the **Close** button.

Importing the Faerûn Chart of Accounts

How to do it...

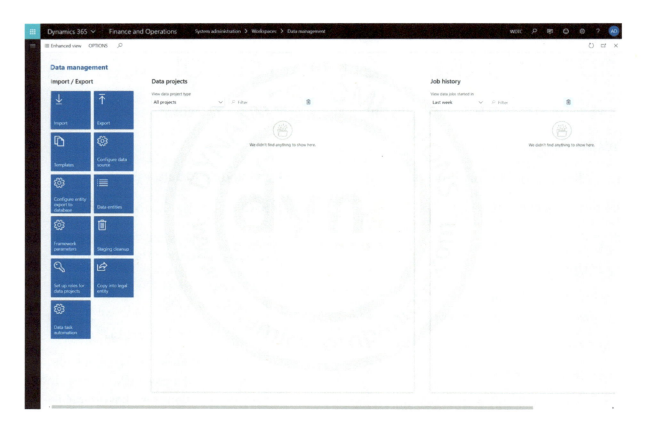

Step 1: Click on the Import button

To do this, we just create a new import job.

To do this just click on the **Import** button.

Importing the Faerûn Chart of Accounts

How to do it...

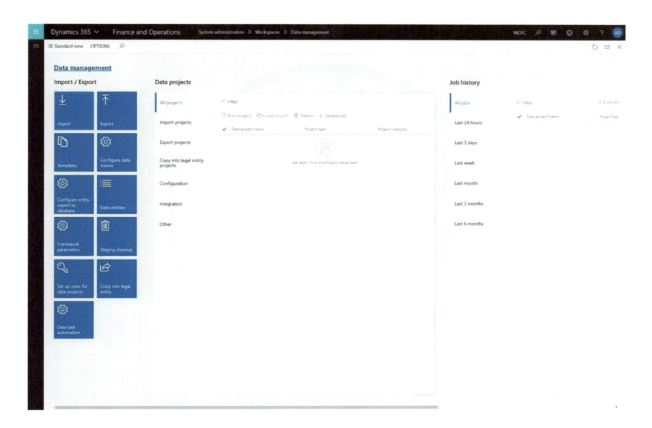

Step 1: Click on the Import button

If we are using the **Enhanced** view for the Data Management tools, then it may look a little different, but we still start the import job the same way.

dync
www.dynamicscompanions.com
Dynamics Companions

- 57 -

www.blindsquirrelpublishing.com
© 2019 Blind Squirrel Publishing, LLC , All Rights Reserved

BLIND SQUIRREL
PUBLISHING

Importing the Faerûn Chart of Accounts

How to do it...

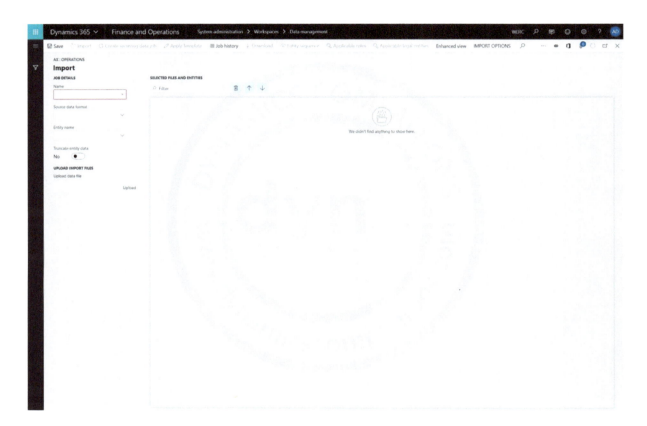

Step 1: Click on the Import button

This will open the Import workspace for us, and we can start configuring the data import.

Importing the Faerûn Chart of Accounts

How to do it...

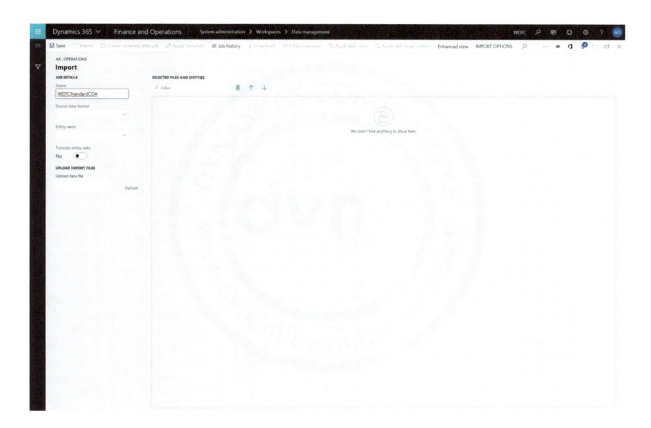

Step 2: Update the Name

We will start off by giving our import job a unique name to identify the import.

To do this, we will just need to change the **Name** value.

For this example, we will want to set the **Name** to **WDTCStandardCOA**.

dync
www.dynamicscompanions.com
Dynamics Companions

- 59 -

www.blindsquirrelpublishing.com
© 2019 Blind Squirrel Publishing, LLC , All Rights Reserved

BLIND SQUIRREL
PUBLISHING

Importing the Faerûn Chart of Accounts

How to do it...

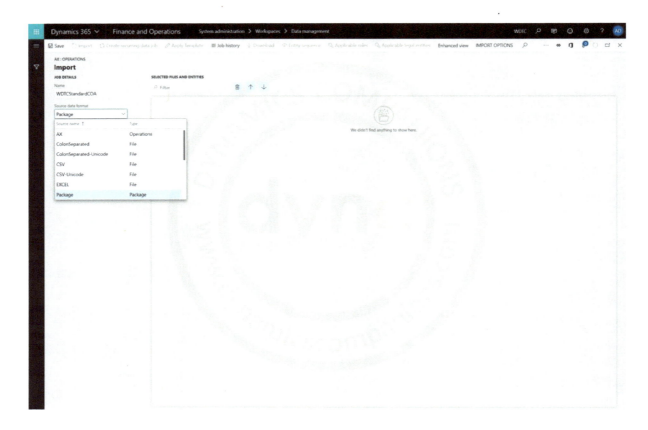

Step 3: Choose the Source data format

We will be importing the chart of accounts data using a zipped-up package that contains all the different entities that we need to set up the Chart of Accounts, so we will want to specify that the import is a Package format.

To do this, we will just need to select the **Source data format** option from the dropdown list.

This time, we will want to click on the **Source data format** dropdown list and select **Package**.

dync
www.dynamicscompanions.com
Dynamics Companions

- 60 -

www.blindsquirrelpublishing.com
© 2019 Blind Squirrel Publishing, LLC , All Rights Reserved

BLIND SQUIRREL
PUBLISHING

Importing the Faerûn Chart of Accounts

How to do it...

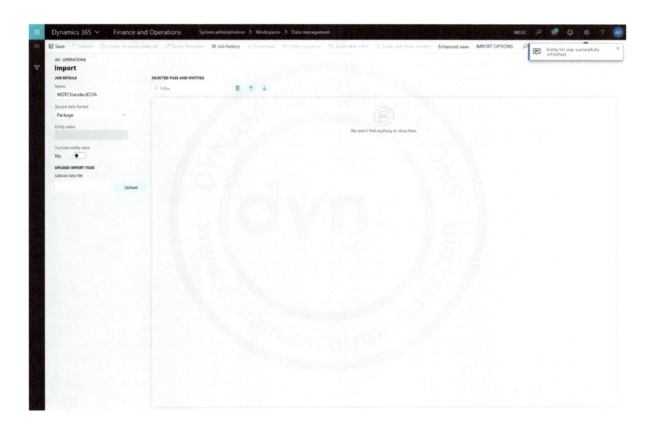

Step 4: Click on the Upload button

Next, we will want to upload the data import package.

To do this, all we need to do is click on the **Upload** button.

Importing the Faerûn Chart of Accounts

How to do it...

Step 5: Click on the Open button

When the File explorer dialog is opened, we just need to navigate to the data package and open it.

To do this, all we need to do is click on the **Open** button.

Importing the Faerûn Chart of Accounts

How to do it...

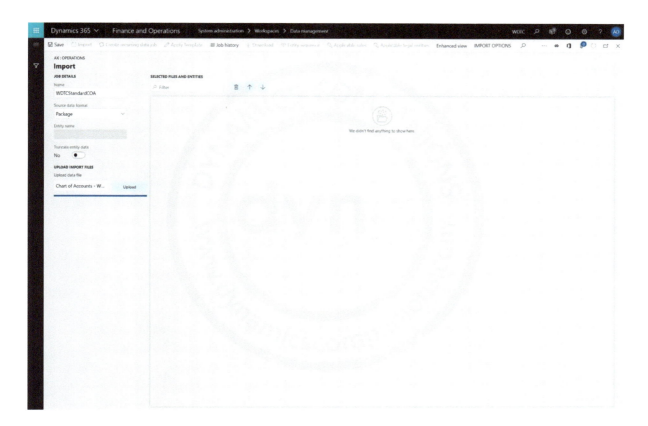

Step 5: Click on the Open button

This will start the importing of the data package.

www.dynamicscompanions.com
Dynamics Companions

- 63 -

www.blindsquirrelpublishing.com
© 2019 Blind Squirrel Publishing, LLC , All Rights Reserved

BLIND SQUIRREL
PUBLISHING

Importing the Faerûn Chart of Accounts

How to do it...

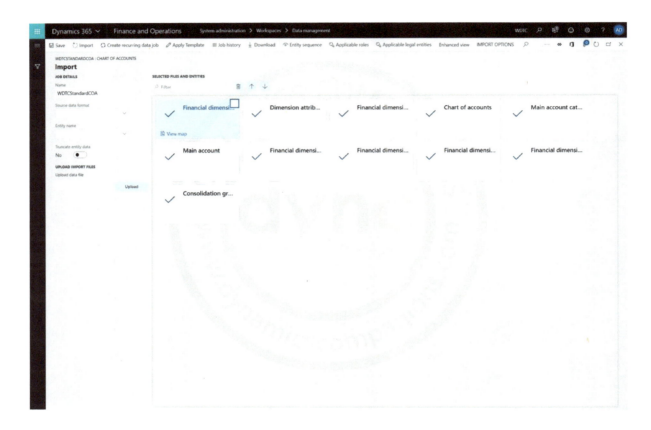

Step 5: Click on the Open button

After a couple of seconds have passed, we will see that eleven different entities were part of the data import package.

www.dynamicscompanions.com
Dynamics Companions

- 64 -

www.blindsquirrelpublishing.com
© 2019 Blind Squirrel Publishing, LLC, All Rights Reserved

BLIND SQUIRREL
PUBLISHING

Importing the Faerûn Chart of Accounts

How to do it...

Step 6: Click on the Import button

If we are in the **Enhanced view,** then it will look a little different, but we will still see that there are eleven different entities that are being imported by this package.

All we need to do now is start the import process.

To do this, all we need to do is click on the **Import** button.

dync
dynamics companions

www.dynamicscompanions.com
Dynamics Companions

- 65 -

www.blindsquirrelpublishing.com
© 2019 Blind Squirrel Publishing, LLC , All Rights Reserved

BLIND SQUIRREL
PUBLISHING

Importing the Faerûn Chart of Accounts

How to do it...

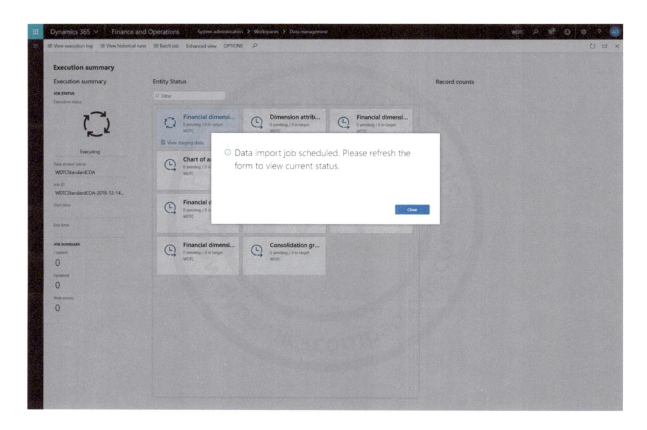

Step 7: Click on the Close button

This will start off a batch job that will import the data in the package for us.

To do this just click on the **Close** button.

dync
www.dynamicscompanions.com
Dynamics Companions

- 66 -

www.blindsquirrelpublishing.com
© 2019 Blind Squirrel Publishing, LLC , All Rights Reserved

BLIND SQUIRREL
PUBLISHING

Importing the Faerûn Chart of Accounts

How to do it...

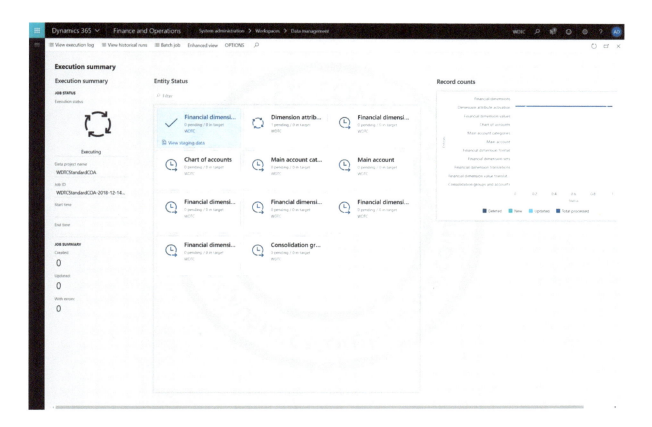

Step 7: Click on the Close button

As the data is importing, we will be able to see the progress of the import as it works through the different data entities.

dync
www.dynamicscompanions.com
Dynamics Companions

- 67 -

www.blindsquirrelpublishing.com
© 2019 Blind Squirrel Publishing, LLC , All Rights Reserved

BLIND SQUIRREL
PUBLISHING

Importing the Faerûn Chart of Accounts

How to do it...

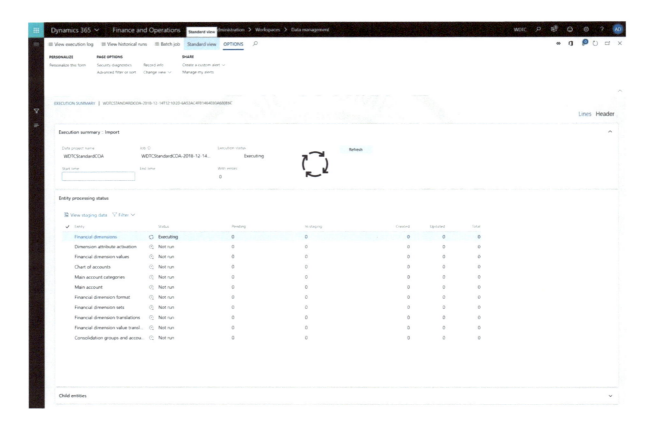

Step 7: Click on the Close button

In the enhanced view we will be able to see the progress as well, including the number of records that are moving from the data import, through the staging tables, and into Dynamics 365.

dync
www.dynamicscompanions.com
Dynamics Companions

- 68 -

www.blindsquirrelpublishing.com
© 2019 Blind Squirrel Publishing, LLC , All Rights Reserved

BLIND SQUIRREL
PUBLISHING

Importing the Faerûn Chart of Accounts

How to do it...

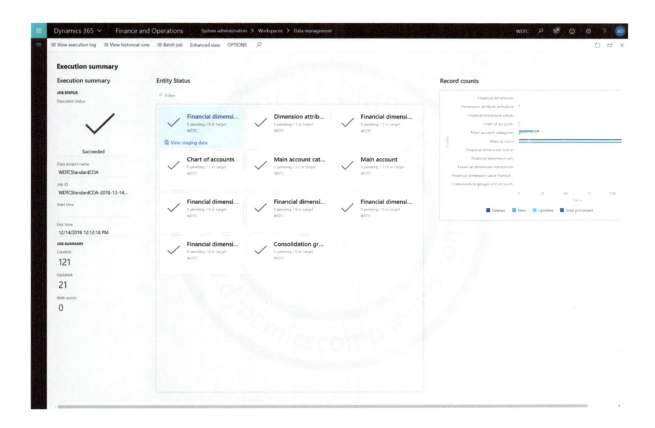

Step 7: Click on the Close button

Eventually, all the data will be imported.

www.dynamicscompanions.com
Dynamics Companions

- 69 -

www.blindsquirrelpublishing.com
© 2019 Blind Squirrel Publishing, LLC , All Rights Reserved

BLIND SQUIRREL
PUBLISHING

Importing the Faerûn Chart of Accounts

How to do it...

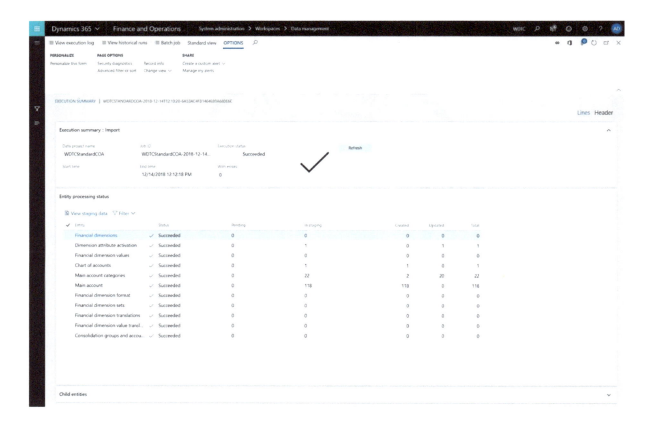

Step 7: Click on the Close button

In the enhanced view we will see the same information.

www.dynamicscompanions.com
Dynamics Companions

- 70 -

www.blindsquirrelpublishing.com
© 2019 Blind Squirrel Publishing, LLC , All Rights Reserved

BLIND SQUIRREL
PUBLISHING

Viewing the Standard Chart of Accounts

Just to make sure that the Chart of accounts has been loaded, we can go and take a look.

How to do it...

Step 1: Open the Chart of accounts form through the menu search

We can find the **Chart of accounts** form is through the menu search feature.

Type in **chart of** into the menu search and select **Chart of accounts**.

Step 2: Click on the Faerûn record

We can see the new Chard of accounts that we just created by selecting the Faerûn Chart of Accounts.

Click on the **Faerûn** record.

If we want, we can drill into the main accounts and see more information.

dync
www.dynamicscompanions.com
Dynamics Companions

- 71 -

www.blindsquirrelpublishing.com
© 2019 Blind Squirrel Publishing, LLC , All Rights Reserved

BLIND SQUIRREL
PUBLISHING

Viewing the Standard Chart of Accounts

How to do it...

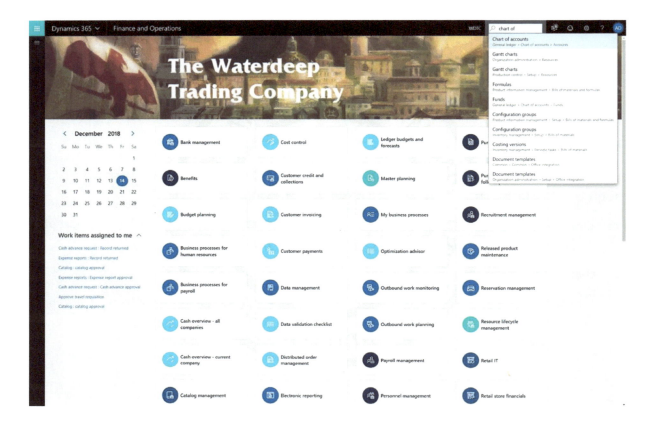

Step 1: Open the Chart of accounts form through the menu search

We can find the **Chart of accounts** form is through the menu search feature.

We can do this by clicking on the search icon in the header of the form (or by pressing **ALT+G**) and then type in **chart of** into the search box. Then you will be able to select the **Chart of accounts** form from the dropdown list.

Viewing the Standard Chart of Accounts

How to do it...

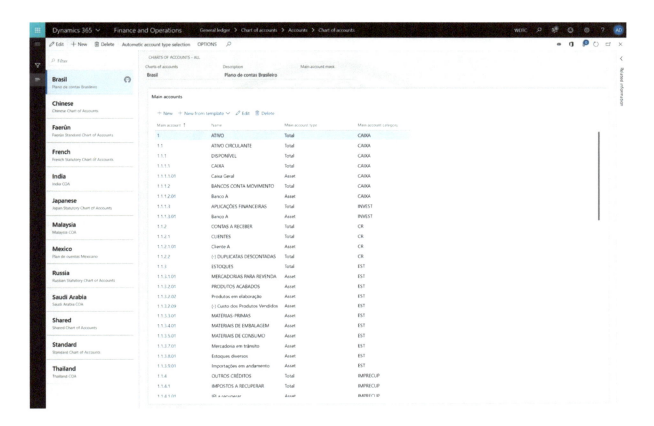

Step 1: Open the Chart of accounts form through the menu search

This will open the Chart of accounts maintenance form where we can see all the different Chart of Account configurations that are configured in the system.

www.dynamicscompanions.com
Dynamics Companions

- 73 -

www.blindsquirrelpublishing.com
© 2019 Blind Squirrel Publishing, LLC , All Rights Reserved

BLIND SQUIRREL
PUBLISHING

Viewing the Standard Chart of Accounts

How to do it...

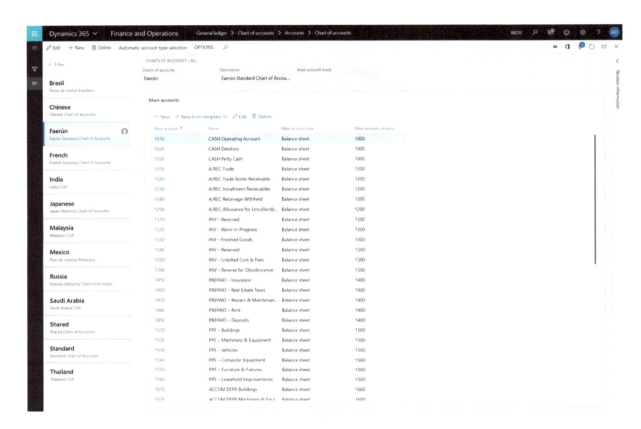

Step 2: Click on the Faerûn record

We can see the new Chard of accounts that we just created by selecting the Faerûn Chart of Accounts.

To do this just click on the **Faerûn** record.

Viewing the Standard Chart of Accounts

How to do it...

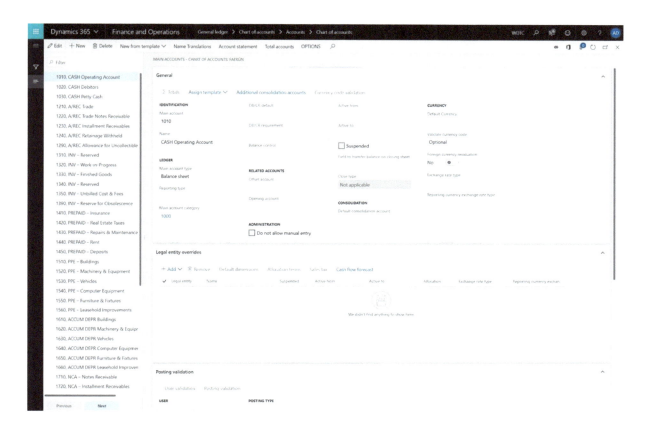

Step 2: Click on the Faerûn record

If we want, we can drill into the main accounts and see more information.

Review

How easy was that? Having the standard Chart of Accounts in an import package saves a lot of time and also makes the initial configuration of the Chard of accounts a breeze.

Creating a new Account structure the Waterdeep Trading Company

Now that we have our new Chart of accounts configured, we can start setting up the Ledger for the **Waterdeep Trading Company** to track all our financial information.

To do this we will need to configure our Account structures that will identify the financial dimensions that we will use in the system, and then link it to our company Ledger.

Topics Covered

- Opening the Account Structures Configuration form

- Creating a new Account Structure

- Activating the Account Structure

- Review

Opening the Account Structures Configuration form

To start off we will want to configure our Account structures and to do that we will need to open the Account structures maintenance form.

How to do it...

Step 1: Open the Configure account structures form through the menu search

We can find the **Configure account structures** form through the menu search feature.

Type in **configure acc** into the menu search and select **Configure account structures**.

Opening the Account Structures Configuration form

How to do it...

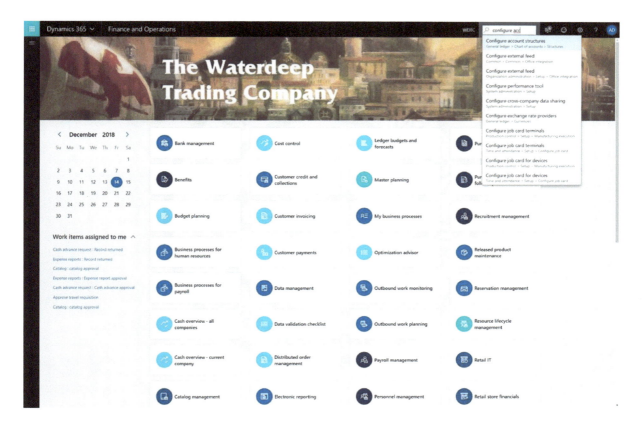

Step 1: Open the Configure account structures form through the menu search

We can find the **Configure account structures** form through the menu search feature.

We can do this by clicking on the search icon in the header of the form (or by pressing **ALT+G**) and then type in **configure acc** into the search box. Then you will be able to select the **Configure account structures** form from the dropdown list.

dync
dynamics companions

www.dynamicscompanions.com
Dynamics Companions

- 79 -

www.blindsquirrelpublishing.com
© 2019 Blind Squirrel Publishing, LLC , All Rights Reserved

BLIND SQUIRREL
PUBLISHING

Opening the Account Structures Configuration form

How to do it...

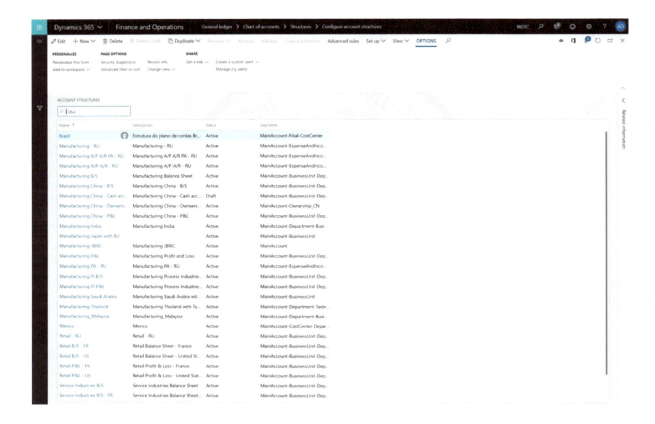

Step 1: Open the Configure account structures form through the menu search

This will open the Account Structures configuration form with all the existing Account structures that are used by the other legal entities.

www.dynamicscompanions.com
Dynamics Companions

- 80 -

www.blindsquirrelpublishing.com
© 2019 Blind Squirrel Publishing, LLC , All Rights Reserved

BLIND SQUIRREL
PUBLISHING

Creating a new Account Structure

Now we will want to create a new Account structure that we will use with our **Waterdeep Trading Company** Ledger.

How to do it...

Step 1: Click on the New button

All we need to do is create a new **Account structure** record.

Click on the **New** button.

Step 2: Update the Account structure

We will give our Account structure a name.

Set the Account structure to Waterdeep Trading Company.

Step 3: Update the Description and click on the Create button

Then we will add a description before we tell the system to create the new Account structure.

Set the Description to Waterdeep Trading Company and click on the Create button.

www.dynamicscompanions.com
Dynamics Companions

- 81 -

www.blindsquirrelpublishing.com
© 2019 Blind Squirrel Publishing, LLC , All Rights Reserved

BLIND SQUIRREL
PUBLISHING

Creating a new Account Structure

How to do it...

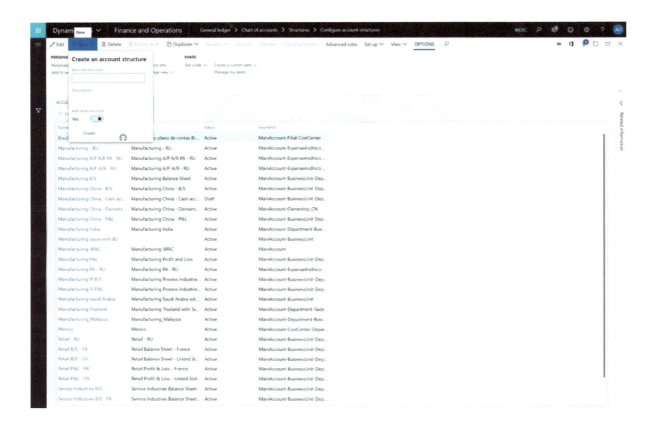

Step 1: Click on the New button

All we need to do is create a new **Account structure** record.

To do this just click on the **New** button.

dync
dynamics companions

www.dynamicscompanions.com
Dynamics Companions

- 82 -

www.blindsquirrelpublishing.com
© 2019 Blind Squirrel Publishing, LLC , All Rights Reserved

BLIND SQUIRREL
PUBLISHING

Creating a new Account Structure

How to do it...

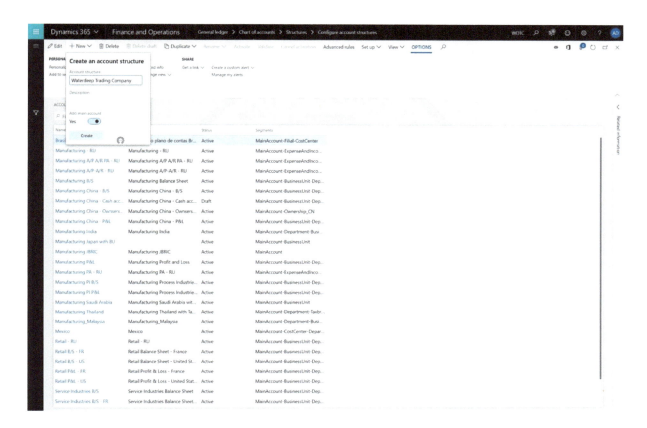

Step 2: Update the Account structure

We will give our Account structure a name.

To do this, we will just need to change the **Account structure** value.

For this example, we will want to set the **Account structure** to **Waterdeep Trading Company**.

dync

www.dynamicscompanions.com
Dynamics Companions

- 83 -

www.blindsquirrelpublishing.com
© 2019 Blind Squirrel Publishing, LLC , All Rights Reserved

BLIND SQUIRREL
PUBLISHING

Creating a new Account Structure

How to do it...

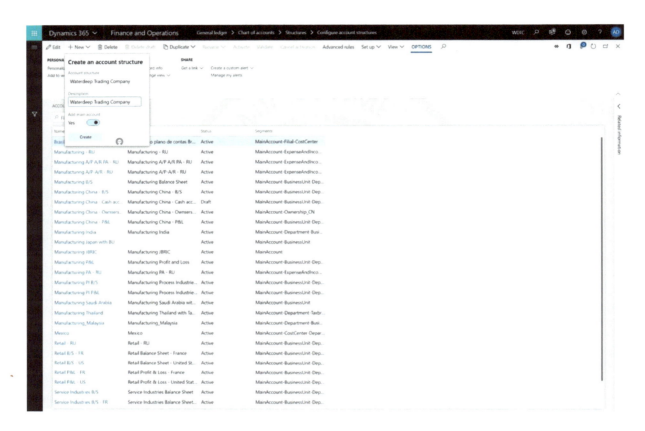

Step 3: Update the Description and click on the Create button

Then we will add a description before we tell the system to create the new Account structure.

To do this just change the **Description** value and click on the **Create** button.

For this example, we will want to set the **Description** to **Waterdeep Trading Company**.

dync
www.dynamicscompanions.com
Dynamics Companions

- 84 -

www.blindsquirrelpublishing.com
© 2019 Blind Squirrel Publishing, LLC , All Rights Reserved

BLIND SQUIRREL
PUBLISHING

Creating a new Account Structure

How to do it...

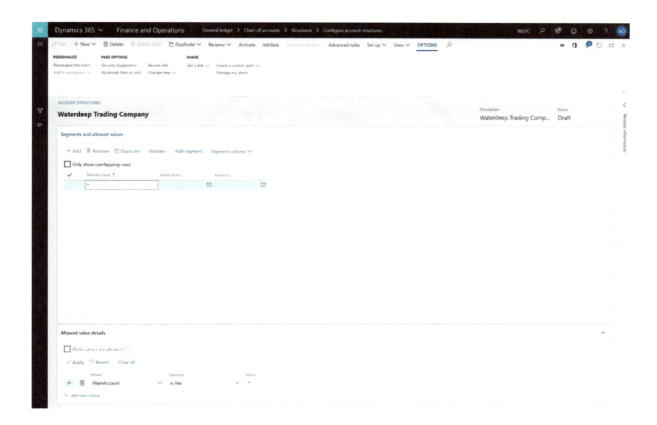

Step 3: Update the Description and click on the Create button

After we have done that, we will see our new Account structure.

www.dynamicscompanions.com
Dynamics Companions

- 85 -

www.blindsquirrelpublishing.com
© 2019 Blind Squirrel Publishing, LLC , All Rights Reserved

BLIND SQUIRREL
PUBLISHING

Activating the Account Structure

Now that we have created our Account structure, we will just need to activate it so that we can use it within our Ledger.

How to do this...

Step 1: Click on the Activate button

So now we just tell the system that we want to Activate the Account Structure.

Click on the **Activate** button.

Step 2: Click on the Activate button

This will open the **Activate account structure** panel, and we can confirm the activation.

Click on the **Activate** button.

Activating the Account Structure

How to do this...

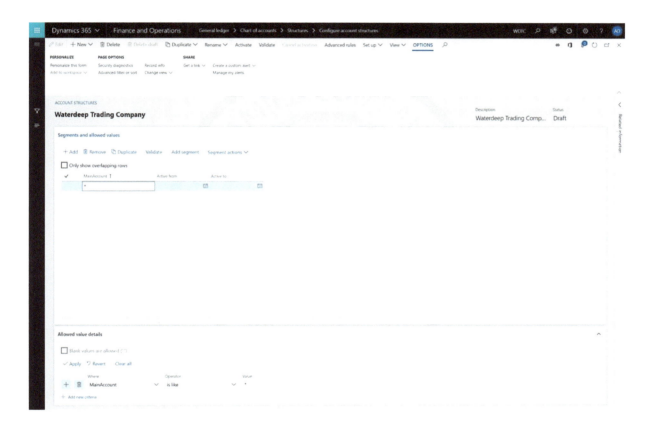

Step 1: Click on the Activate button

So now we just tell the system that we want to Activate the Account Structure.

To do this, all we need to do is click on the **Activate** button.

www.dynamicscompanions.com
Dynamics Companions

- 87 -

www.blindsquirrelpublishing.com
© 2019 Blind Squirrel Publishing, LLC , All Rights Reserved

BLIND SQUIRREL
PUBLISHING

Activating the Account Structure

How to do this...

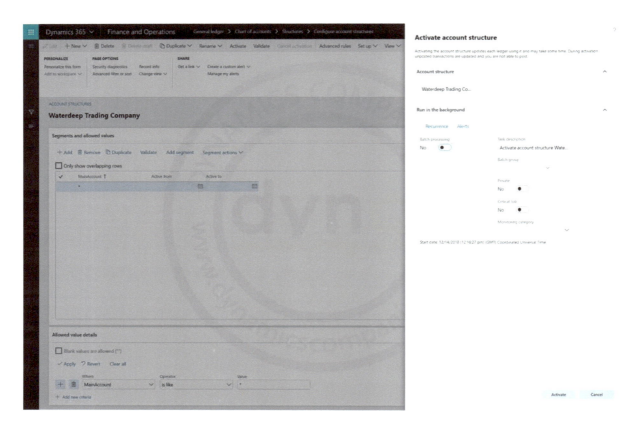

Step 2: Click on the Activate button

This will open the **Activate account structure** panel, and we can confirm the activation.

To do this just click on the **Activate** button.

www.dynamicscompanions.com
Dynamics Companions

- 88 -

www.blindsquirrelpublishing.com
© 2019 Blind Squirrel Publishing, LLC , All Rights Reserved

BLIND SQUIRREL
PUBLISHING

Activating the Account Structure

How to do this...

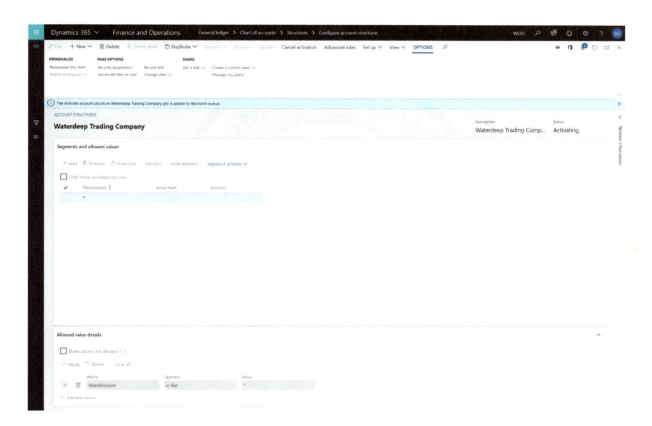

Step 2: Click on the Activate button

This will start the activation process, and we will see that the **Status** is **Activating,** and then change to **Active**.

dync
www.dynamicscompanions.com
Dynamics Companions

- 89 -

www.blindsquirrelpublishing.com
© 2019 Blind Squirrel Publishing, LLC , All Rights Reserved

BLIND SQUIRREL
PUBLISHING

Review

Congratulations. Now we have all the building blocks that we need to continue and set up our ledger.

Configuring the Ledger for the Waterdeep Trading Company

Now that we have the Chard of Accounts configured, and our Account Structure defined for the **Waterdeep Trading Company** we can move on and set up our ledger for the company.

Topics Covered

- Opening the Ledger Maintenance form

- Configuring the Ledger

- Viewing the Main Accounts for the Waterdeep Trading Company

- Review

Opening the Ledger Maintenance form

To do this we will want to open up the **Ledger** configuration form.

How to do it...

Step 1: Open the Ledger form through the menu search

We can find the **Ledger** form is through the menu search feature.

Type in **ledger** into the menu search and select **Ledger**.

Opening the Ledger Maintenance form

How to do it...

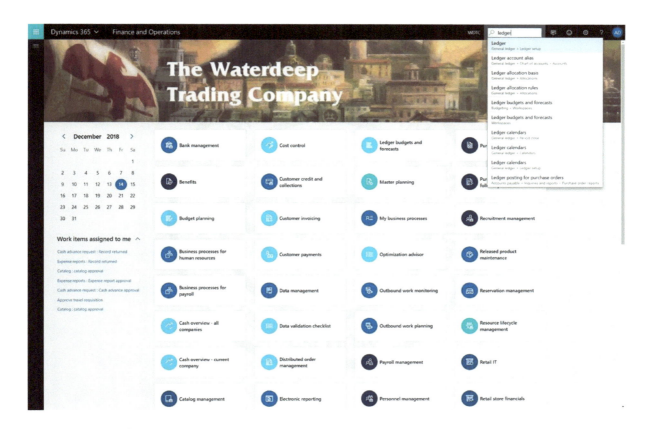

Step 1: Open the Ledger form through the menu search

We can find the **Ledger** form is through the menu search feature.

We can do this by clicking on the search icon in the header of the form (or by pressing **ALT+G**) and then type in **ledger** into the search box. Then you will be able to select the **Ledger** form from the dropdown list.

dync
www.dynamicscompanions.com
Dynamics Companions

- 93 -

www.blindsquirrelpublishing.com
© 2019 Blind Squirrel Publishing, LLC , All Rights Reserved

BLIND SQUIRREL
PUBLISHING

Opening the Ledger Maintenance form

How to do it...

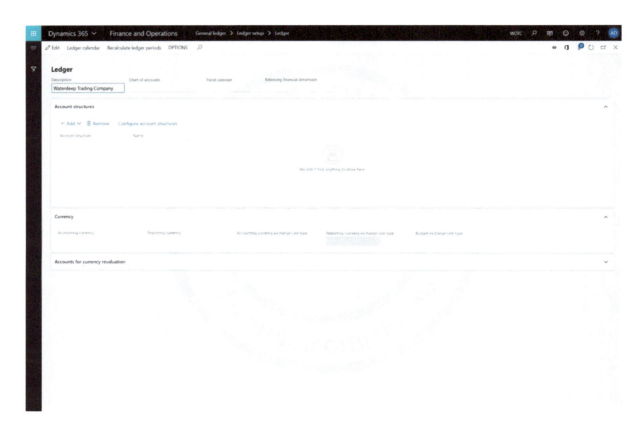

Step 1: Open the Ledger form through the menu search

This will open the ledger details for the **Waterdeep Trading Company** legal entity, and we will see that there is a little bit that needs to be configured.

Configuring the Ledger

Now let's tie all the items together and configure the Ledger.

How to do it...

Step 1: Click on the Edit button

To start off, we will want to switch to Edit mode within the Ledger configuration.

Click on the **Edit** button.

Step 2: Choose the Chart of accounts

We will start off by setting the Chard of Accounts to be the new Chart of accounts that we imported earlier.

Click on the **Chart of accounts** dropdown list And choose **Faerûn**.

Step 3: Choose the Fiscal calendar

We will then want to select a Fiscal calendar that we want to use within the legal entity.

Click on the **Fiscal calendar** dropdown list And select **Cal**.

Step 4: Select the Accounting currency

We will want to specify that we want to track the ledger in FGP as the base currency.

Click on the **Accounting currency** dropdown list And select **FGP**.

Step 5: Select the Reporting currency

Also, we will report all our financials in FGP as well.

Click on the **Reporting currency** dropdown list And select **FGP**.

Step 6: Choose the Accounting currency exchange rate

We will want to set the default exchange rate provider to be the Faerûn exchange rate calculations.

Click on the **Accounting currency exchange rate** dropdown list And choose **Faerûn**.

Step 7: Select the Budget exchange rate type

And we will also want to use the same exchange rate type for the budgeting calculations.

Click on the **Budget exchange rate type** dropdown list And select **Faerûn**.

Step 8: Click on the Add button

Finally, we will want to select the account structure that we will use for the **Waterdeep Trading Company** ledger.

Click on the **Add** button.

www.dynamicscompanions.com
Dynamics Companions

- 95 -

www.blindsquirrelpublishing.com
© 2019 Blind Squirrel Publishing, LLC , All Rights Reserved

BLIND SQUIRREL
PUBLISHING

Step 9: Select the Waterdeep Trading Company record and click on the Select button

This will allow us to select the **Waterdeep Trading Company** account structure that we configured earlier.

Select the **Waterdeep Trading Company** record and click on the **Select** button.

Step 10: Click on the Yes button

We will get a notice telling us that we are about to add an account structure which is OK to accept.

Click on the **Yes** button.

Configuring the Ledger

How to do it...

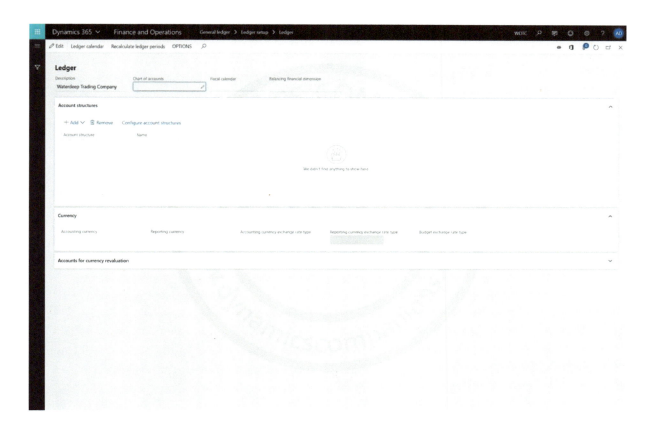

Step 1: Click on the Edit button

To start off, we will want to switch to Edit mode within the Ledger configuration.

To do this just click on the **Edit** button.

www.dynamicscompanions.com
Dynamics Companions

- 97 -

www.blindsquirrelpublishing.com
© 2019 Blind Squirrel Publishing, LLC , All Rights Reserved

BLIND SQUIRREL
PUBLISHING

Configuring the Ledger

How to do it...

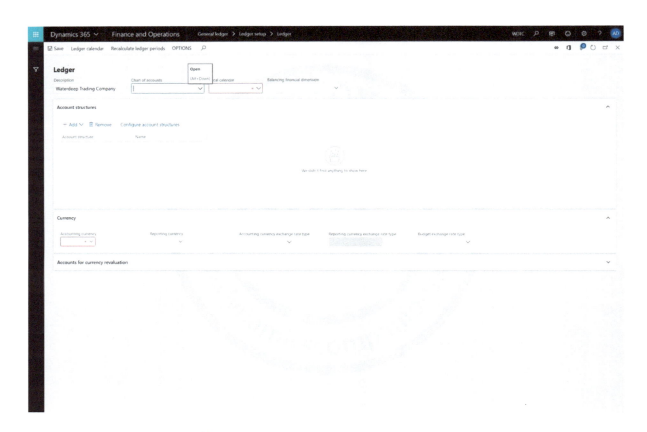

Step 1: Click on the Edit button

This will allow us to maintain all the different elements of the Ledger.

www.dynamicscompanions.com
Dynamics Companions

- 98 -

www.blindsquirrelpublishing.com
© 2019 Blind Squirrel Publishing, LLC , All Rights Reserved

BLIND SQUIRREL
PUBLISHING

Configuring the Ledger

How to do it...

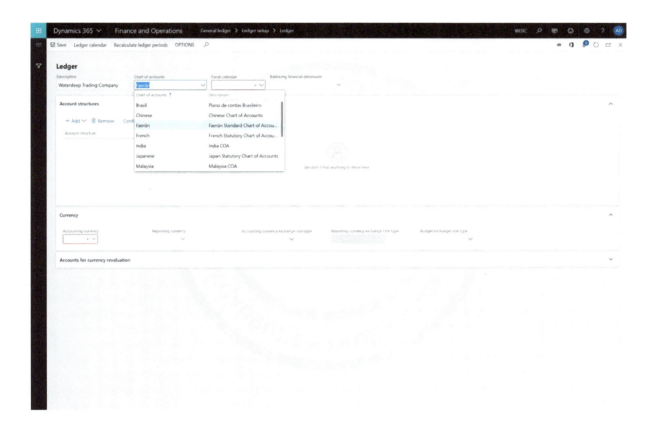

Step 2: Choose the Chart of accounts

We will start off by setting the Chard of Accounts to be the new Chart of accounts that we imported earlier.

To do this just select the **Chart of accounts** value from the dropdown list.

This time, we will want to click on the **Chart of accounts** dropdown list and pick **Faerûn**.

www.dynamicscompanions.com
Dynamics Companions

- 99 -

www.blindsquirrelpublishing.com
© 2019 Blind Squirrel Publishing, LLC , All Rights Reserved

BLIND SQUIRREL
PUBLISHING

Configuring the Ledger

How to do it...

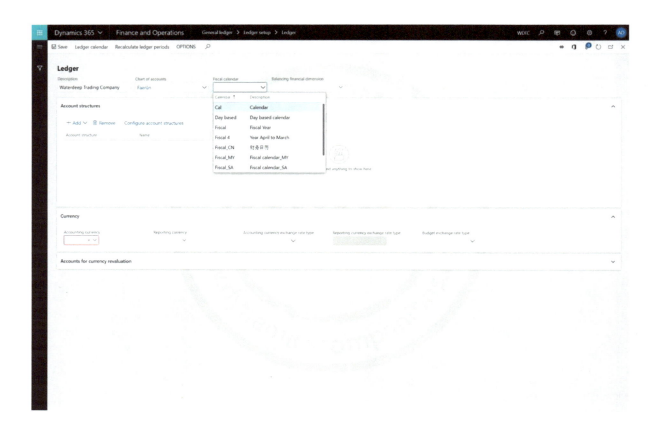

Step 3: Choose the Fiscal calendar

We will then want to select a Fiscal calendar that we want to use within the legal entity.

To do this, we will just need to pick the **Fiscal calendar** option from the dropdown list.

For this example, we will want to click on the **Fiscal calendar** dropdown list and select **Cal**.

Configuring the Ledger

How to do it...

Step 4: Select the Accounting currency

We will want to specify that we want to track the ledger in FGP as the base currency.

To do this just select the **Accounting currency** option from the dropdown list.

For this example, we will want to click on the **Accounting currency** dropdown list and pick **FGP**.

www.dynamicscompanions.com
Dynamics Companions

- 101 -

www.blindsquirrelpublishing.com
© 2019 Blind Squirrel Publishing, LLC , All Rights Reserved

BLIND SQUIRREL
PUBLISHING

Configuring the Ledger

How to do it...

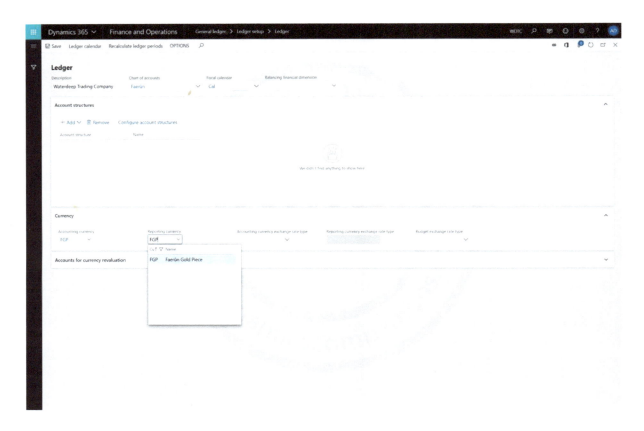

Step 5: Select the Reporting currency

Also, we will report all our financials in FGP as well.

To do this just select the **Reporting currency** value from the dropdown list.

This time, we will want to click on the **Reporting currency** dropdown list and select **FGP**.

www.dynamicscompanions.com
Dynamics Companions

- 102 -

www.blindsquirrelpublishing.com
© 2019 Blind Squirrel Publishing, LLC , All Rights Reserved

BLIND SQUIRREL
PUBLISHING

Configuring the Ledger

How to do it...

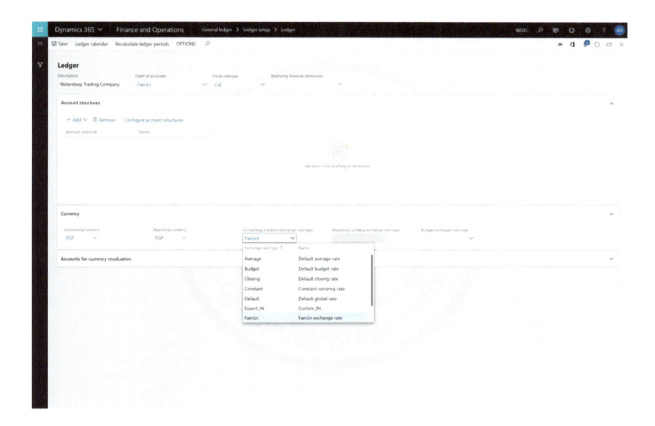

Step 6: Choose the Accounting currency exchange rate

We will want to set the default exchange rate provider to be the Faerûn exchange rate calculations.

To do this, we will just need to select the **Accounting currency exchange rate** option from the dropdown list.

This time, we will want to click on the **Accounting currency exchange rate** dropdown list and select **Faerûn**.

dync
dynamics companions
www.dynamicscompanions.com
Dynamics Companions

- 103 -

www.blindsquirrelpublishing.com
© 2019 Blind Squirrel Publishing, LLC , All Rights Reserved

BLIND SQUIRREL
PUBLISHING

Configuring the Ledger

How to do it...

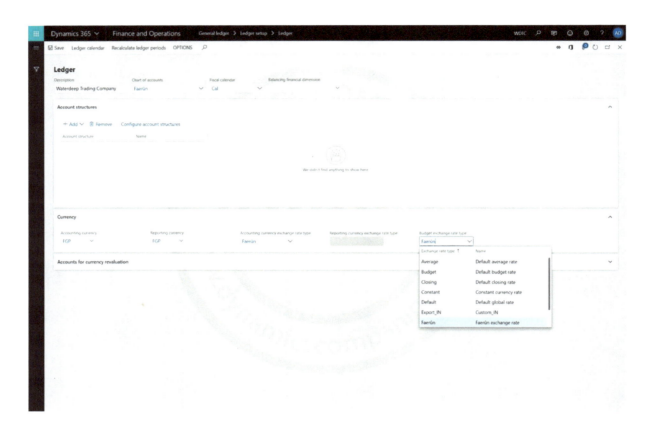

Step 7: Select the Budget exchange rate type

And we will also want to use the same exchange rate type for the budgeting calculations.

To do this just select the **Budget exchange rate type** option from the dropdown list.

For this example, we will want to click on the **Budget exchange rate type** dropdown list and pick **Faerûn**.

Configuring the Ledger

How to do it...

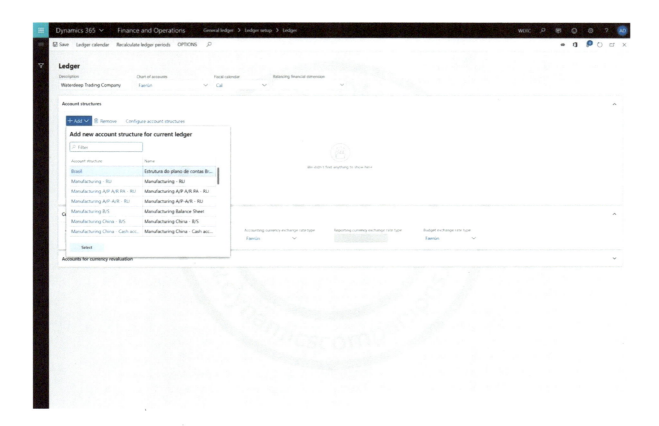

Step 8: Click on the Add button

Finally, we will want to select the account structure that we will use for the **Waterdeep Trading Company** ledger.

To do this, all we need to do is click on the **Add** button.

Configuring the Ledger

How to do it...

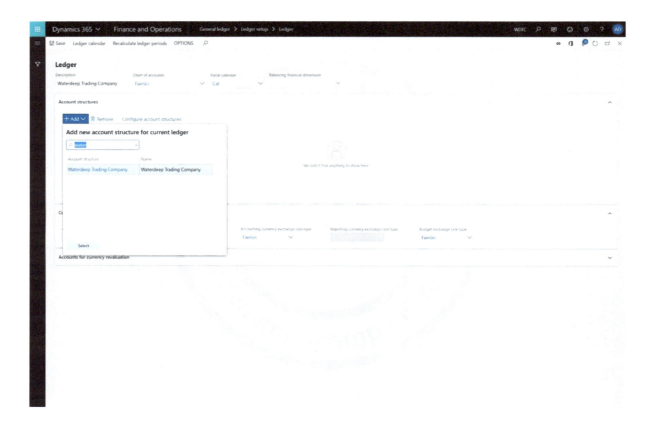

Step 9: Select the Waterdeep Trading Company record and click on the Select button

This will allow us to select the **Waterdeep Trading Company** account structure that we configured earlier.

To do this, all we need to do is select the **Waterdeep Trading Company** record and click on the **Select** button.

www.dynamicscompanions.com
Dynamics Companions

- 106 -

www.blindsquirrelpublishing.com
© 2019 Blind Squirrel Publishing, LLC , All Rights Reserved

BLIND SQUIRREL
PUBLISHING

Configuring the Ledger

How to do it...

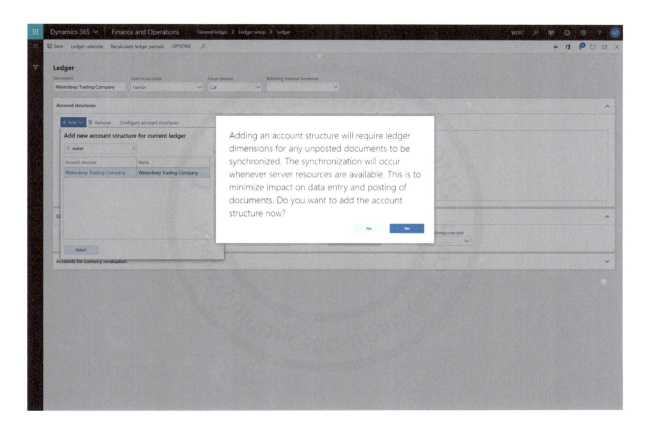

Step 10: Click on the Yes button

We will get a notice telling us that we are about to add an account structure which is OK to accept.

To do this, all we need to do is click on the **Yes** button.

www.dynamicscompanions.com
Dynamics Companions

- 107 -

www.blindsquirrelpublishing.com
© 2019 Blind Squirrel Publishing, LLC , All Rights Reserved

BLIND SQUIRREL
PUBLISHING

Configuring the Ledger

How to do it...

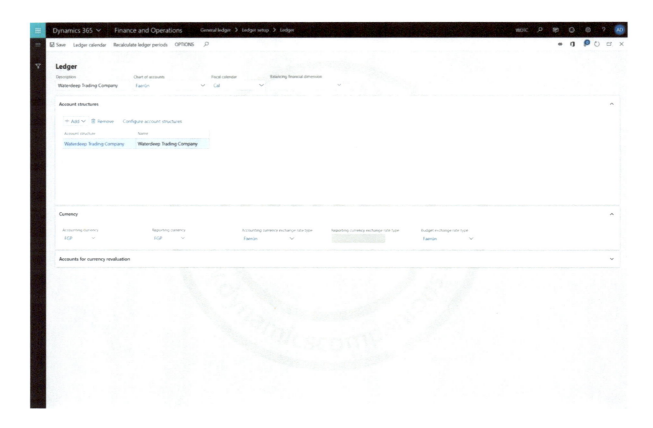

Step 10: Click on the Yes button

After we have done that our ledger is configured.

Viewing the Main Accounts for the Waterdeep Trading Company

Now that the Ledger is configured, we can check out all our new main accounts that are linked to the Ledger and the Legal Entity.

How to do it...

Step 1: Open the Main accounts form through the menu search

We can find the **Main accounts** form is through the menu search feature.

Type in **main accounts** into the menu search and select **Main accounts**.

Viewing the Main Accounts for the Waterdeep Trading Company

How to do it...

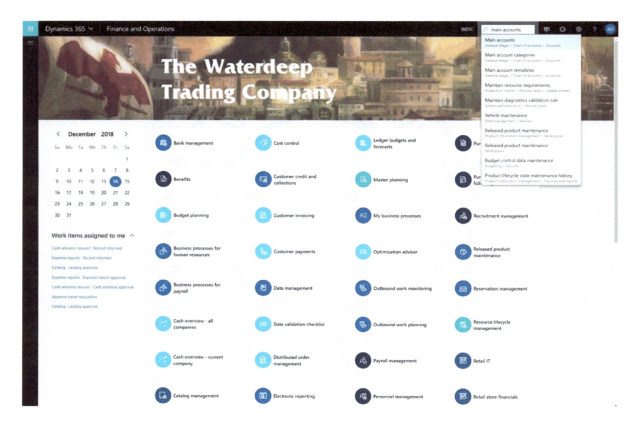

Step 1: Open the Main accounts form through the menu search

We can find the **Main accounts** form is through the menu search feature.

We can do this by clicking on the search icon in the header of the form (or by pressing **ALT+G**) and then type in **main accounts** into the search box. Then you will be able to select the **Main accounts** form from the dropdown list.

www.dynamicscompanions.com
Dynamics Companions

- 110 -

www.blindsquirrelpublishing.com
© 2019 Blind Squirrel Publishing, LLC , All Rights Reserved

BLIND SQUIRREL
PUBLISHING

Viewing the Main Accounts for the Waterdeep Trading Company

How to do it...

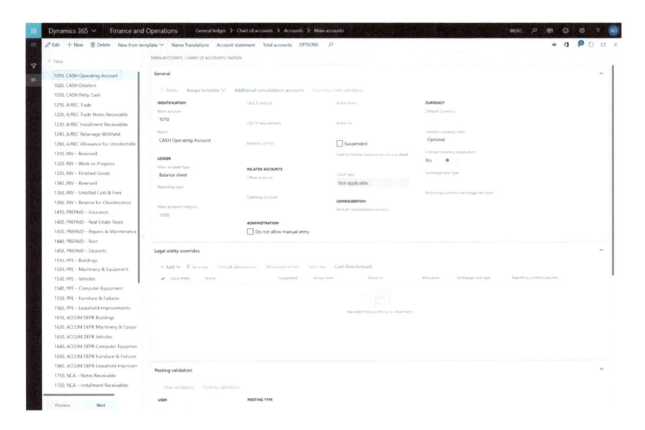

Step 1: Open the Main accounts form through the menu search

Now we will see all the accounts that are linked to the legal entity and the ledger.

www.dynamicscompanions.com
Dynamics Companions

- 111 -

www.blindsquirrelpublishing.com
© 2019 Blind Squirrel Publishing, LLC , All Rights Reserved

BLIND SQUIRREL
PUBLISHING

Review

How easy was that. Now we have a ledger.

Creating an Operating Bank Account

Now that we have our Ledger configured, we will want to finish off the setup if the company by creating a Bank Account that we will associate with the legal entity to track all our money.

Topics Covered

- Opening up the Bank management form

- Adding a new Bank Account

- Associating the Bank Account to the Legal Entity

- Review

Opening up the Bank management form

To do this we will want to open the **Bank accounts** maintenance form.

How to do it...

Step 1: Open the Bank accounts form through the menu search

We can find the **Bank accounts** form is through the menu search feature.

Type in **bank acc** into the menu search and select **Bank accounts**.

dync
www.dynamicscompanions.com
Dynamics Companions

- 114 -

www.blindsquirrelpublishing.com
© 2019 Blind Squirrel Publishing, LLC , All Rights Reserved

Opening up the Bank management form

How to do it...

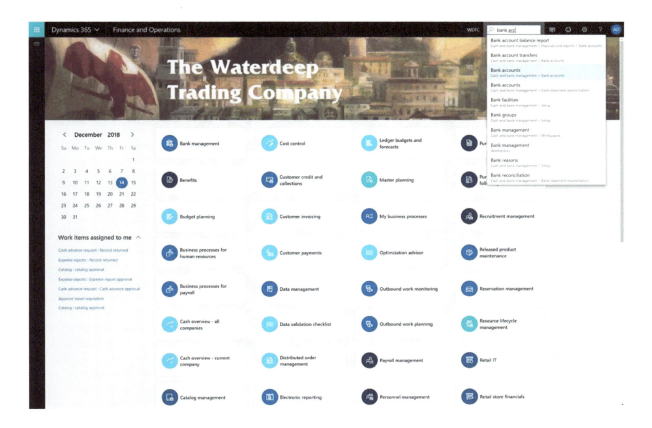

Step 1: Open the Bank accounts form through the menu search

We can find the **Bank accounts** form is through the menu search feature.

We can do this by clicking on the search icon in the header of the form (or by pressing **ALT+G**) and then type in **bank acc** into the search box. Then you will be able to select the **Bank accounts** form from the dropdown list.

dync
www.dynamicscompanions.com
Dynamics Companions

- 115 -

www.blindsquirrelpublishing.com
© 2019 Blind Squirrel Publishing, LLC , All Rights Reserved

BLIND SQUIRREL
PUBLISHING

Opening up the Bank management form

How to do it...

Step 1: Open the Bank accounts form through the menu search

This will open the **Bank account** maintenance form where we will be able to set up as many different bank accounts as we like.

Adding a new Bank Account

Let's create our first Bank account to track all of the operating cash that we have.

How to do it...

Step 1: Click on the New button

To do this, we will want to create a new Bank Account record,

Click on the **New** button.

Step 2: Update the Bank account

We will start off by giving the bank account a code to identify it.

Set the Bank account to FBOF.

Step 3: Update the Routing number

Next, we will specify the Routing number for the bank account.

Set the Routing number to 1234567890.

Step 4: Update the Bank account number

And then we will add the bank account number.

Set the Bank account number to 00001.

Step 5: Select the Main account

Next, we will select the main account within the ledger that the bank account will be tracked against.

Click on the Main account dropdown list And select 1010 (CASH Operating Account).

Step 6: Update the Name

And finally, we will give a more descriptive name for the bank account.

Set the Name to First Bank of Faerûn.

www.dynamicscompanions.com
Dynamics Companions

- 117 -

www.blindsquirrelpublishing.com
© 2019 Blind Squirrel Publishing, LLC , All Rights Reserved

BLIND SQUIRREL
PUBLISHING

Adding a new Bank Account

How to do it...

Step 1: Click on the New button

To do this, we will want to create a new Bank Account record,

To do this, all we need to do is click on the **New** button.

Adding a new Bank Account

How to do it...

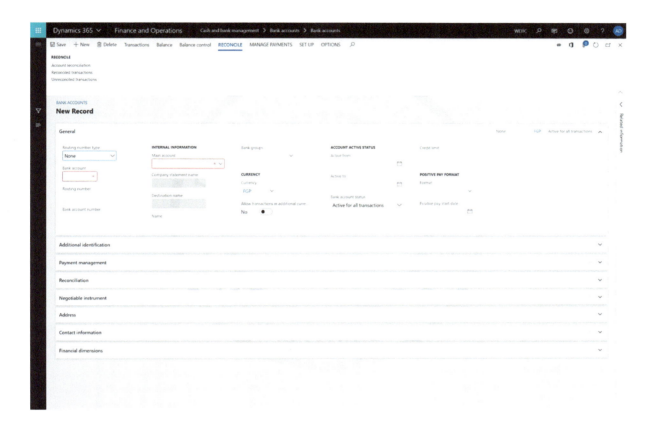

Step 1: Click on the New button

This will create a new Bank Account record for us.

dync
www.dynamicscompanions.com
Dynamics Companions

- 119 -

www.blindsquirrelpublishing.com
© 2019 Blind Squirrel Publishing, LLC , All Rights Reserved

BLIND SQUIRREL
PUBLISHING

Adding a new Bank Account

How to do it...

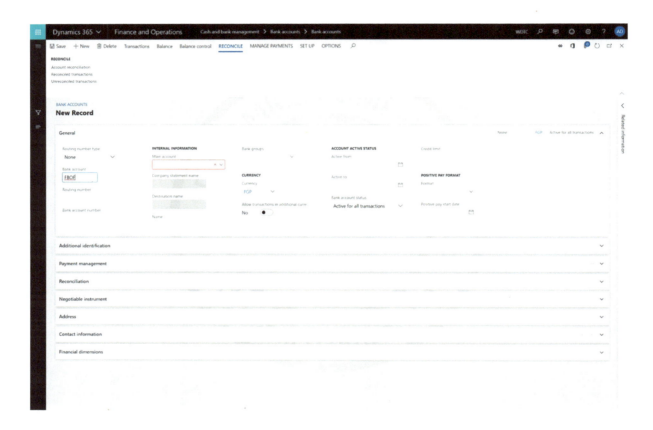

Step 2: Update the Bank account

We will start off by giving the bank account a code to identify it.

To do this just change the **Bank account** value.

This time, we will want to set the **Bank account** to **FBOF**.

www.dynamicscompanions.com
Dynamics Companions

- 120 -

www.blindsquirrelpublishing.com
© 2019 Blind Squirrel Publishing, LLC , All Rights Reserved

BLIND SQUIRREL
PUBLISHING

Adding a new Bank Account

How to do it...

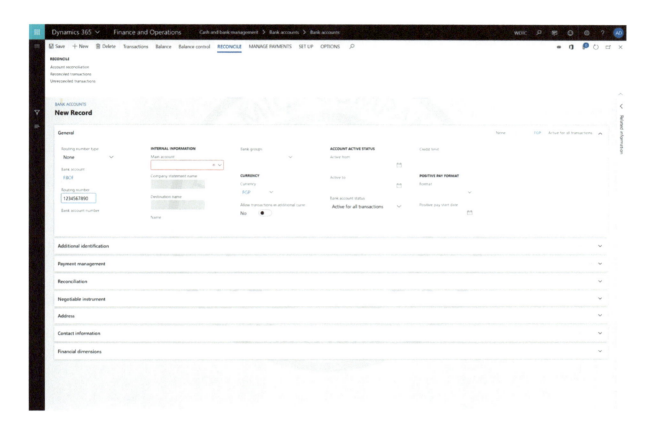

Step 3: Update the Routing number

Next, we will specify the Routing number for the bank account.

To do this, we will just need to update the **Routing number** value.

This time, we will want to set the **Routing number** to **1234567890**.

www.dynamicscompanions.com
Dynamics Companions

- 121 -

www.blindsquirrelpublishing.com
© 2019 Blind Squirrel Publishing, LLC , All Rights Reserved

BLIND SQUIRREL
PUBLISHING

Adding a new Bank Account

How to do it...

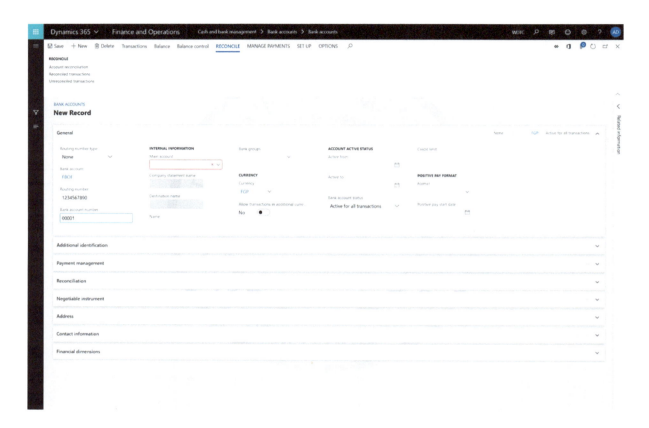

Step 4: Update the Bank account number

And then we will add the bank account number.

To do this just change the **Bank account number** value.

This time, we will want to set the **Bank account number** to **00001**.

dync
dynamics companions

www.dynamicscompanions.com
Dynamics Companions

- 122 -

www.blindsquirrelpublishing.com
© 2019 Blind Squirrel Publishing, LLC , All Rights Reserved

BLIND SQUIRREL
PUBLISHING

Adding a new Bank Account

How to do it...

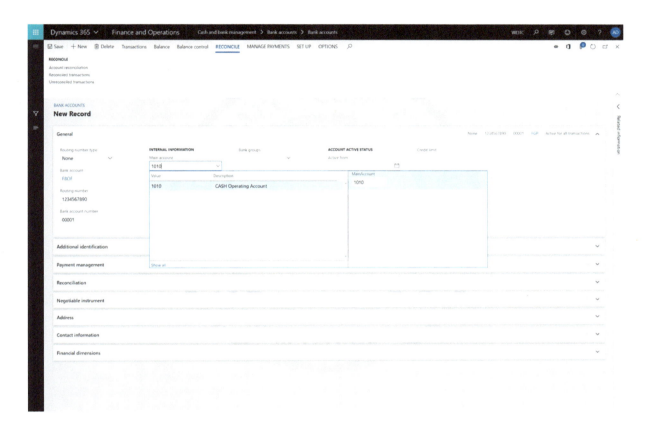

Step 5: Select the Main account

Next, we will select the main account within the ledger that the bank account will be tracked against.

To do this just select the **Main account** value from the dropdown list.

This time, we will want to click on the **Main account** dropdown list and select **1010 (CASH Operating Account)**.

www.dynamicscompanions.com
Dynamics Companions

- 123 -

www.blindsquirrelpublishing.com
© 2019 Blind Squirrel Publishing, LLC , All Rights Reserved

BLIND SQUIRREL
PUBLISHING

Adding a new Bank Account

How to do it...

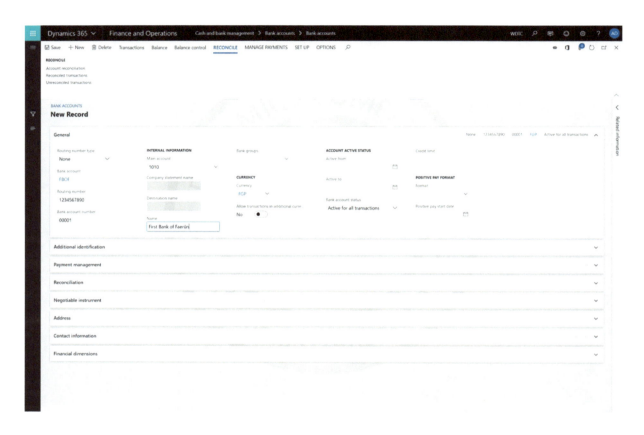

Step 6: Update the Name

And finally, we will give a more descriptive name for the bank account.

To do this just update the **Name** value.

For this example, we will want to set the **Name** to **First Bank of Faerûn**.

Adding a new Bank Account

How to do it...

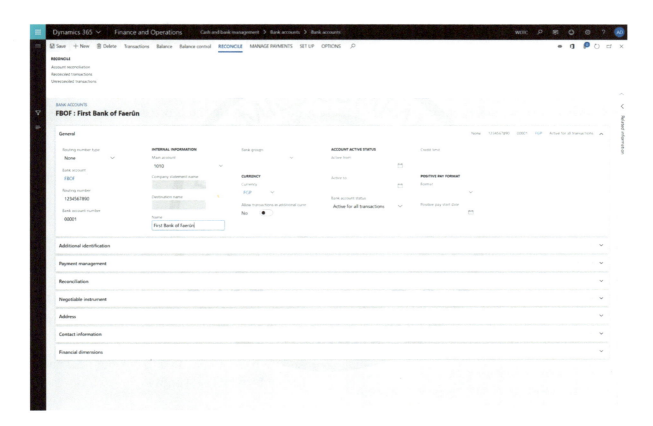

Step 6: Update the Name

After we have done that, our Bank account is configured.

www.dynamicscompanions.com
Dynamics Companions

- 125 -

www.blindsquirrelpublishing.com
© 2019 Blind Squirrel Publishing, LLC , All Rights Reserved

BLIND SQUIRREL
PUBLISHING

Associating the Bank Account to the Legal Entity

Now that we have our Bank Account configured, there is one last step in the process, and that is to associate the Bank Account with our Legal entity.

How to do it...

Step 1: Open the Legal entities form through the menu search

We return to the **Legal entities** form by searching for it using the menu search feature.

Type in **legal** into the menu search and select **Legal entities**.

Step 2: Expand Bank account information tab

To update the Bank account information for the legal entity, we will want to go to the **Bank account information** fast tab.

Expand the Bank account information tab.

Step 3: Click on the Edit button

To update the bank account information we will need to switch to edit mode.

Click on the **Edit** button.

Step 4: Update the Routing number

We will now be able to update the default routing number for the bank accounts.

Set the Routing number to 1234567890.

Step 5: Choose the Bank account

And then we will be able to link our new bank account to the Legal entity.

Click on the **Bank account** dropdown list And choose **FBOF (First Bank of Faerûn)**.

Step 6: Click on the Save button

Now we can save the changes, and we are done configuring the Legal entity.

Click on the **Save** button.

Associating the Bank Account to the Legal Entity

How to do it...

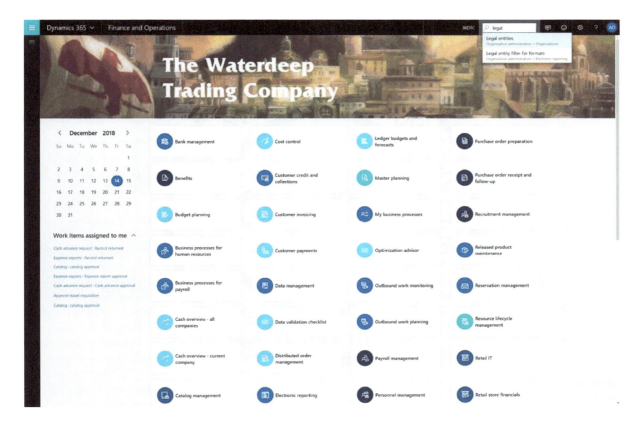

Step 1: Open the Legal entities form through the menu search

We return to the **Legal entities** form by searching for it using the menu search feature.

We can do this by clicking on the search icon in the header of the form (or by pressing **ALT+G**) and then type in **legal** into the search box. Then you will be able to select the **Legal entities** form from the dropdown list.

dync
www.dynamicscompanions.com
Dynamics Companions

- 127 -

www.blindsquirrelpublishing.com
© 2019 Blind Squirrel Publishing, LLC , All Rights Reserved

BLIND SQUIRREL
PUBLISHING

Associating the Bank Account to the Legal Entity

How to do it...

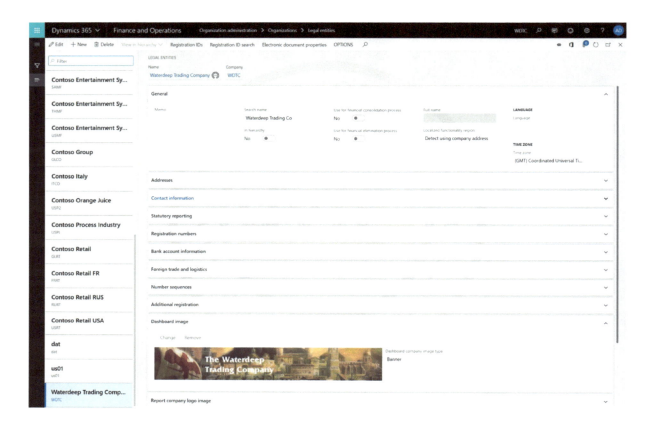

Step 1: Open the Legal entities form through the menu search

This will open up the **Legal entities** form, and we should be within the **Waterdeep Trading Company** legal entity .

Associating the Bank Account to the Legal Entity

How to do it...

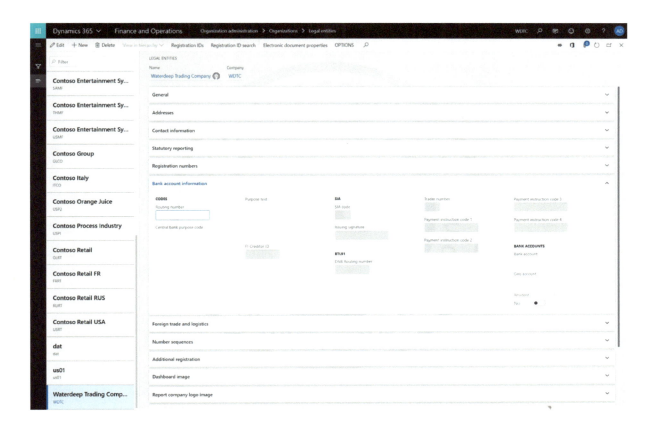

Step 2: Expand Bank account information tab

To update the Bank account information for the legal entity, we will want to go to the **Bank account information** fast tab.

To do this just expand the **Bank account information** tab.

www.dynamicscompanions.com
Dynamics Companions

- 129 -

www.blindsquirrelpublishing.com
© 2019 Blind Squirrel Publishing, LLC , All Rights Reserved

BLIND SQUIRREL
PUBLISHING

Associating the Bank Account to the Legal Entity

How to do it...

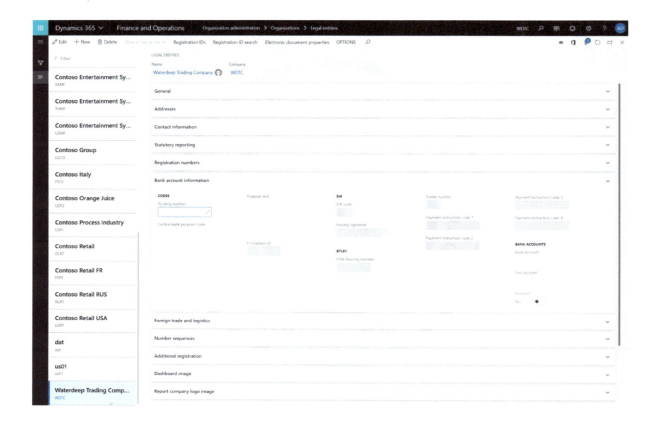

Step 3: Click on the Edit button

To update the bank account information we will need to switch to edit mode.

To do this, all we need to do is click on the **Edit** button.

dync
dynamics companions

www.dynamicscompanions.com
Dynamics Companions

- 130 -

www.blindsquirrelpublishing.com
© 2019 Blind Squirrel Publishing, LLC , All Rights Reserved

BLIND SQUIRREL
PUBLISHING

Associating the Bank Account to the Legal Entity

How to do it...

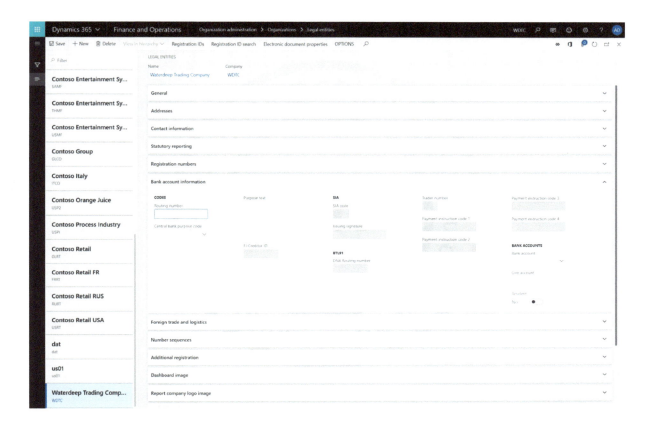

Step 3: Click on the Edit button

This will allow us to update the Bank account information.

www.dynamicscompanions.com
Dynamics Companions

www.blindsquirrelpublishing.com
© 2019 Blind Squirrel Publishing, LLC , All Rights Reserved

BLIND SQUIRREL
PUBLISHING

Associating the Bank Account to the Legal Entity

How to do it...

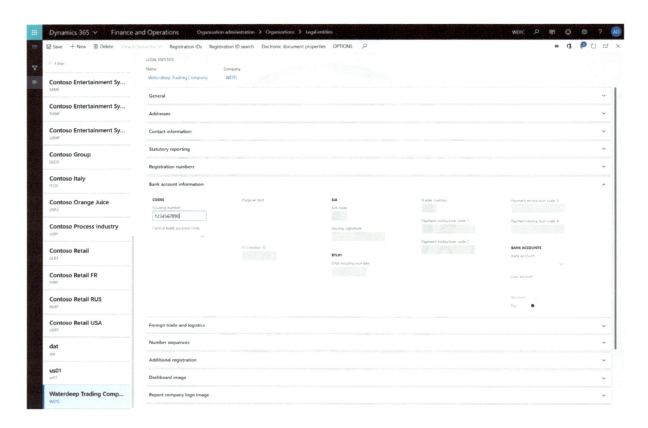

Step 4: Update the Routing number

We will now be able to update the default routing number for the bank accounts.

To do this, we will just need to update the **Routing number** value.

This time, we will want to set the **Routing number** to **1234567890**.

www.dynamicscompanions.com
Dynamics Companions

- 132 -

www.blindsquirrelpublishing.com
© 2019 Blind Squirrel Publishing, LLC , All Rights Reserved

BLIND SQUIRREL
PUBLISHING

Associating the Bank Account to the Legal Entity

How to do it...

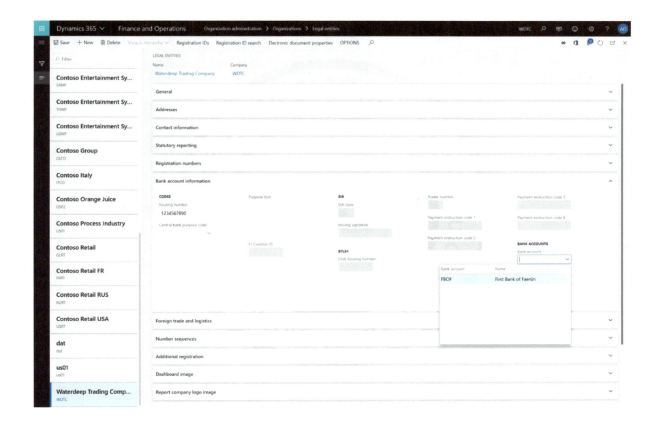

Step 5: Choose the Bank account

And then we will be able to link our new bank account to the Legal entity.

To do this, we will just need to select the **Bank account** option from the dropdown list.

This time, we will want to click on the **Bank account** dropdown list and select **FBOF (First Bank of Faerûn)**.

www.dynamicscompanions.com
Dynamics Companions

- 133 -

www.blindsquirrelpublishing.com
© 2019 Blind Squirrel Publishing, LLC , All Rights Reserved

BLIND SQUIRREL
PUBLISHING

Associating the Bank Account to the Legal Entity

How to do it...

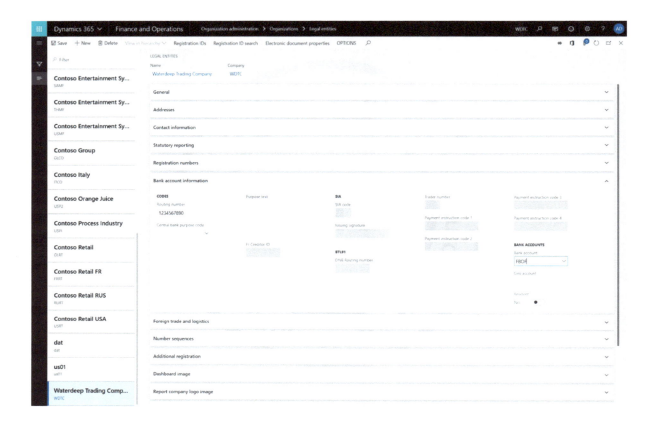

Step 6: Click on the Save button

Now we can save the changes, and we are done configuring the Legal entity.

To do this just click on the **Save** button.

Review

How simple was that? We set up a new bank account to manage all our Operating account coinage and linked it to the Legal entity.

Setting the Waterdeep Trading Company as the default legal entity

Before we finish this module, we will make one final tweak to the system, and that is to set the **Waterdeep Trading Company** as the default legal entity for our user.

This will make the system automatically use the **Waterdeep Trading Company** when we log into the system, and we won't have to switch from the DAT company to WDTC each time.

Topics Covered

- Opening the User Options

- Updating the User preferences

- Review

Opening the User Options

To do this we will need to go to the User settings within Dynamics 365.

How to do it...

Step 1: Click on the User options menu item

Click on the **User options** menu item within the settings menu.

Opening the User Options

How to do it...

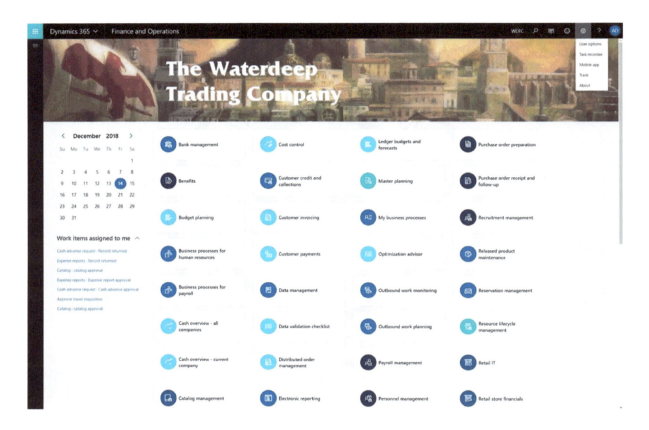

Step 1: Click on the User options menu item

To do this, all we need to do is click on the **User options** menu item within the settings menu.

Opening the User Options

How to do it...

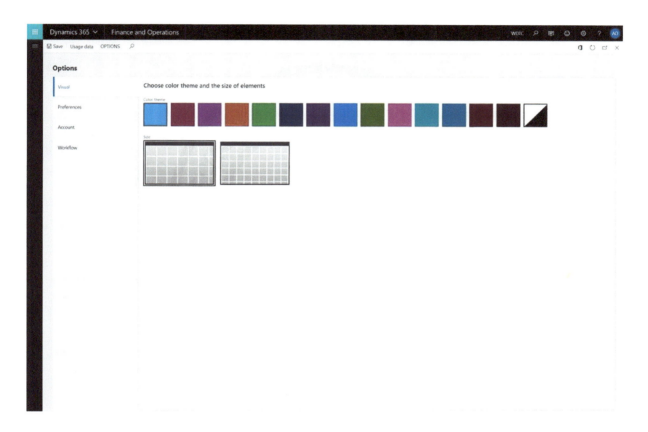

Step 1: Click on the User options menu item

This will open up our users' options where we can tweak some of the user defaults.

www.dynamicscompanions.com
Dynamics Companions

- 139 -

www.blindsquirrelpublishing.com
© 2019 Blind Squirrel Publishing, LLC , All Rights Reserved

BLIND SQUIRREL
PUBLISHING

Updating the User preferences

Now we will want to update the users' preferences.

How to do it...

Step 1: Select the Preferences tab

To do this, we will want to switch to see the User Preferences within the User settings.

Select the **Preferences** tab.

Step 2: Select the Company

Now we can change the default company that the user will be started in when we log into Dynamics 365.

Click on the **Company** dropdown list And select **WDTC**.

Step 3: Select the Country/region

While we are here, we can also change the default Country that we will use whenever we need to configure addresses.

Click on the **Country/region** dropdown list And choose **FAE**.

Step 4: Click on the Save button

After we have done that, we are done and can save the user preferences.

Click on the **Save** button.

Updating the User preferences

How to do it...

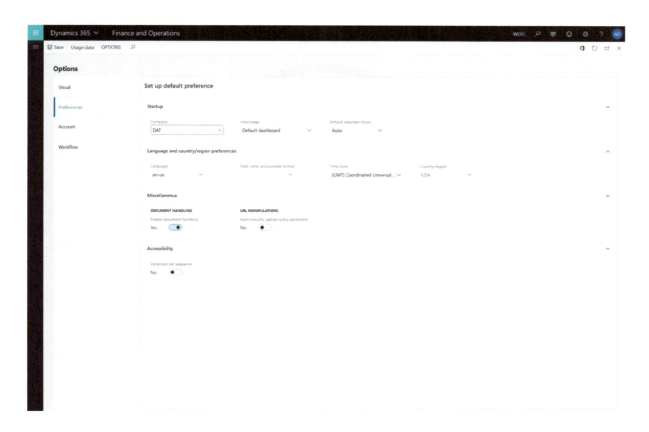

Step 1: Select the Preferences tab

To do this, we will want to switch to see the User Preferences within the User settings.

To do this, all we need to do is select the **Preferences** tab.

www.dynamicscompanions.com
Dynamics Companions

- 141 -

www.blindsquirrelpublishing.com
© 2019 Blind Squirrel Publishing, LLC , All Rights Reserved

BLIND SQUIRREL
PUBLISHING

Updating the User preferences

How to do it...

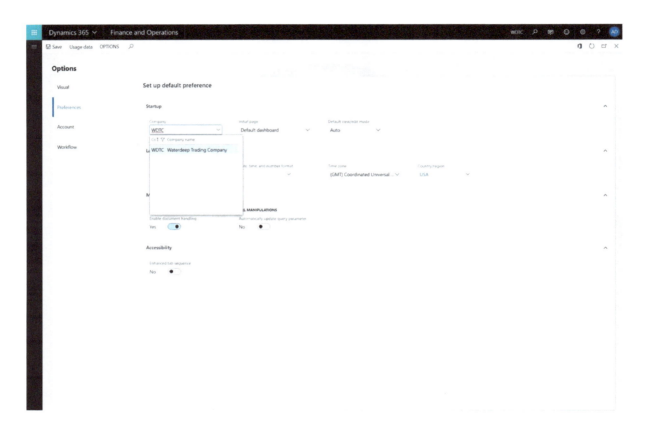

Step 2: Select the Company

Now we can change the default company that the user will be started in when we log into Dynamics 365.

To do this just select the **Company** value from the dropdown list.

For this example, we will want to click on the **Company** dropdown list and pick **WDTC**.

Updating the User preferences

How to do it...

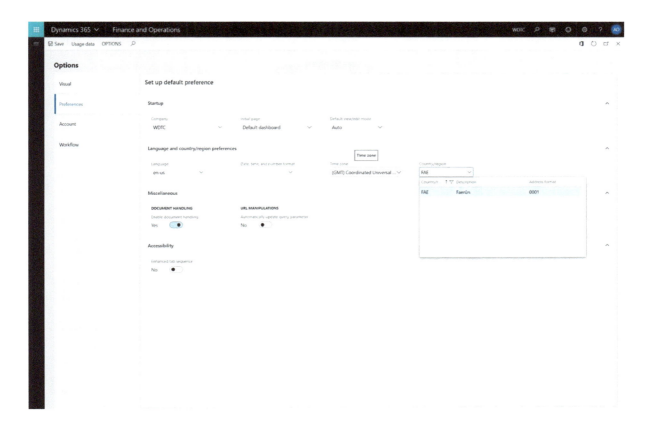

Step 3: Select the Country/region

While we are here, we can also change the default Country that we will use whenever we need to configure addresses.

To do this just select the **Country/region** option from the dropdown list.

This time, we will want to click on the **Country/region** dropdown list and pick **FAE**.

www.dynamicscompanions.com
Dynamics Companions

- 143 -

www.blindsquirrelpublishing.com
© 2019 Blind Squirrel Publishing, LLC , All Rights Reserved

BLIND SQUIRREL
PUBLISHING

Updating the User preferences

How to do it...

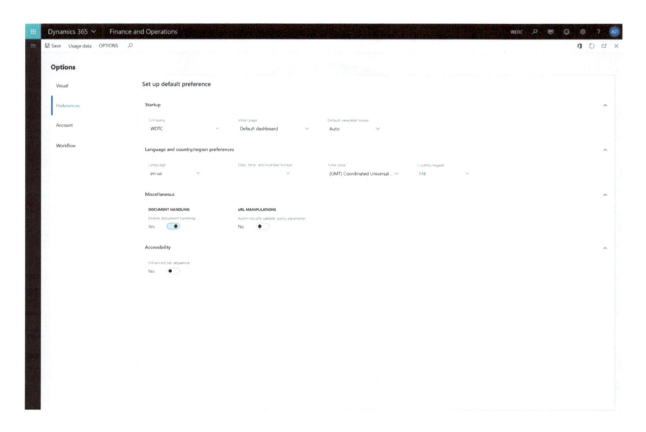

Step 4: Click on the Save button

After we have done that, we are done and can save the user preferences.

To do this, all we need to do is click on the **Save** button.

Review

This is a small tweak to the user options, but it will save a couple of clicks each time we log into Dynamics 365.

Updating the Fiscal Calendar

The Fiscal calendars within Dynamics 365 track all of the financial periods and dates associated with the accounting system.

Unfortunately the calendars that were set up within our system are a little out of date and don't have the current fiscal year for **1495 DR - The Year of the Tyrant's Pawn** (2019 EY) set up within the fiscal calendar.

So we need to update our Fiscal Calendars a little.

Topics Covered

- Adding a new year to the Fiscal Calendar

Adding a new year to the Fiscal Calendar

Right now we will want to access the Fiscal Calendars so that we can add a new Fiscal Year.

Topics Covered

- Opening the Fiscal Calendar maintenance form

- Adding a new year to the Fiscal Calendar

dync
dynamics companions
www.dynamicscompanions.com
Dynamics Companions

- 147 -

www.blindsquirrelpublishing.com
© 2019 Blind Squirrel Publishing, LLC , All Rights Reserved

BLIND SQUIRREL
PUBLISHING

Opening the Fiscal Calendar maintenance form

To do this we will want to find the **Fiscal calendar** maintenance form.

How to do it...

Step 1: Open the Fiscal calendars form through the menu search

We can find the **Fiscal calendars** form through the menu search feature.

We can do this by clicking on the search icon in the header of the form (or by pressing **ALT+G**) and then type in **fiscal cal** into the search box.

Then you will be able to select the **Fiscal calendars** form from the dropdown list.

This will open up the current Fiscal calendar that is linked to the **Waterdeep Trading Company's** legal entity, and sure enough, we don't have the current fiscal year for **1495 DR - The Year of the Tyrant's Pawn.**

Opening the Fiscal Calendar maintenance form

How to do it...

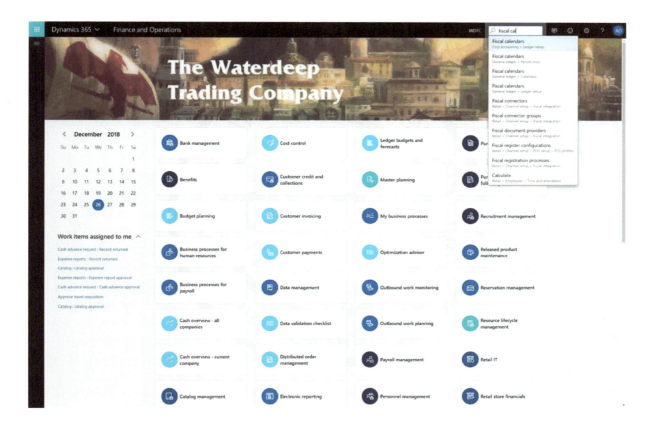

Step 1: Open the Fiscal calendars form through the menu search

We can find the **Fiscal calendars** form through the menu search feature.

We can do this by clicking on the search icon in the header of the form (or by pressing **ALT+G**) and then type in **fiscal cal** into the search box. Then you will be able to select the **Fiscal calendars** form from the dropdown list.

dync
www.dynamicscompanions.com
Dynamics Companions

- 149 -

www.blindsquirrelpublishing.com
© 2019 Blind Squirrel Publishing, LLC , All Rights Reserved

BLIND SQUIRREL
PUBLISHING

Opening the Fiscal Calendar maintenance form

How to do it...

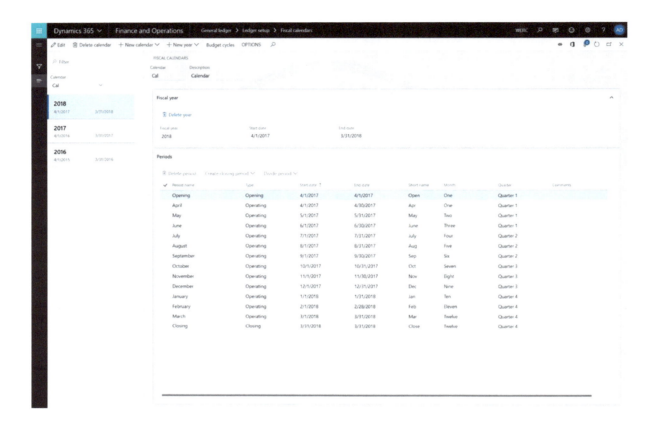

Step 1: Open the Fiscal calendars form through the menu search

This will open up the current Fiscal calendar that is linked to the **Waterdeep Trading Company's** legal entity, and sure enough, we don't have the current fiscal year for **1495 DR - The Year of the Tyrant's Pawn.**

dync
www.dynamicscompanions.com
Dynamics Companions

- 150 -

www.blindsquirrelpublishing.com
© 2019 Blind Squirrel Publishing, LLC , All Rights Reserved

BLIND SQUIRREL
PUBLISHING

Adding a new year to the Fiscal Calendar

Now we will want to add a new year to the current calendar.

How to do it...

Step 1: Click on the New Year button and click on the Create button

The good thing is that we don't need to add each of the years periods by hand, we can use the **New Year** wizard to create them for us.

To do this, all we need to do is click on the **New Year** button and click on the **Create** button.

This will create a brand new Fiscal calendar year for us matching the format of the prior years.

dync
www.dynamicscompanions.com
Dynamics Companions

- 151 -

www.blindsquirrelpublishing.com
© 2019 Blind Squirrel Publishing, LLC , All Rights Reserved

BLIND SQUIRREL
PUBLISHING

Adding a new year to the Fiscal Calendar

How to do it...

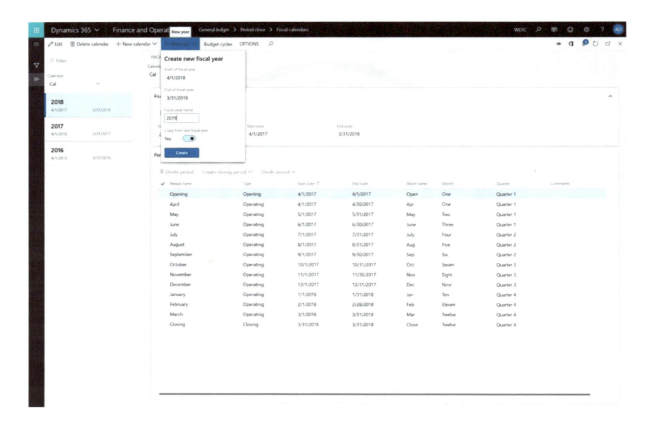

Step 1: Click on the New Year button and click on the Create button

The good thing is that we don't need to add each of the years periods by hand, we can use the **New Year** wizard to create them for us.

To do this, all we need to do is click on the **New Year** button and click on the **Create** button.

Adding a new year to the Fiscal Calendar

How to do it...

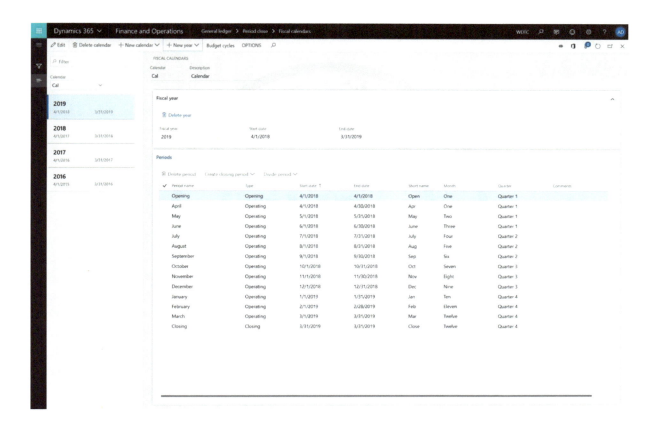

Step 1: Click on the New Year button and click on the Create button

This will create a brand new Fiscal calendar year for us matching the format of the prior years.

dync
www.dynamicscompanions.com
Dynamics Companions

- 153 -

www.blindsquirrelpublishing.com
© 2019 Blind Squirrel Publishing, LLC , All Rights Reserved

BLIND SQUIRREL
PUBLISHING

Review

Great. Now you know how to manage the fiscal calendars within Dynamics 365, and we have a new year that we will be posting all of our transactions into.

You won't have to do this again until **1496 DR - The Year of the Duplicitous Courtier** rolls around.

Summary

Congratulations. We have created a new standard Chart of Accounts for the **Waterdeep Trading Company**, we have defined our account structures and linked them to the company's ledger, and we have set up a new bank account and linked it to the Legal Entity.

That wasn't too hard don't you think?

Now we can move on and start tracking our business.

About The Author

Murray Fife is an Author of over 25 books on Microsoft Dynamics including the Bare Bones Configuration Guide series of over 15 books which step the user through the setup of initial Dynamics instance, then through the Financial modules and then through the configuration of the more specialized modules like production, service management, and project accounting. You can find all his books on Amazon at **www.amazon.com/author/murrayfife**.

For more information on Murray, here is his contact information:

If you are interested in contacting Murray or want to follow his blogs and posts then here is all of his contact information:

Email: murray@murrayfife.com

Twitter: @murrayfife

Facebook: faceook.com/murraycfife

Google: google.com/+murrayfife

LinkedIn: linkedin.com/in/murrayfife

Blog: atinkerersnotebook.com

SlideShare: slideshare.net/murrayfife

Amazon: amazon.com/author/murrayfife